My Brother Tom

My Brother Tom

Bill Petite

My Brother Tom

KDP Amazon Publishing
Bill Petite
bill4theos@yahoo.com

Table of Contents

Brothers aren't simply close; brothers are knit together. -Robert Rivers

Introduction

Since Adam and Eve were created by God and they began to populate the earth, brothers have always existed. Although it's hopeful the vast number of brothers who would follow the birth of Cain and Abel did not have the same type of ending. But I'm sure there were some. Having a brother who you are close to is a lifetime experience which can never be replaced. You can have many sisters but it's just not the same. You can be close to a sister but it's just not the same.

Brothers do things which sisters will not want to do and sisters will attempt to get you to do stuff you don't want to do. Brothers, most times, relate to each other and experience similar things in life. My brother and I were always close. Even after a fight, we would soon be doing something together again and the fight was forgotten. We stood up for each other and played different sports together when we could. We shared similar interests but still had our own which the other didn't care for.

When brothers are close, it's a bond that can be very difficult to break, if at all. When two brothers are best friends, that bond will never be broken and it will last a lifetime. Don't ever take a brother for granted or ignore his need for attention regardless of the issue. A brother needs your support and will always be there to return that gesture.

I had four brothers but my younger brother and I were the closest and mostly because of the age differences. We were closer than veneer on wood and if one was in need, the other was there. We shared heartbreaks and times of joy. Our parents treated us as individuals and never showed favoritism to one or the other.

This is a story about my brother Tom who died recently. It will talk about his life and how he lived it. It's a story about a man who was so much better in so many ways than his brother. I encourage you to read this book with your brother in mind, if you have one. Never in this life was anyone able to separate my brother from me until that day the Lord took him home. But it's only temporary because one day I will join him in the place Jesus has prepared for us. There's nothing that compares to a brother who you are very close to.

The Early Years

My brother Tom was born in Latrobe PA on September 28, 1952. I wasn't quite two years old yet so I don't remember anything about that. My mother was 32 when I was born and almost 35 when Tom was born. So, we were the last of the children in our family. My mother always told us that I was planned but Tom was an accident. But she never insinuated that Tom was an unwanted child. It was exactly the opposite because he was the baby of the family and got more than enough attention. Since Tom and I were only about twenty-two months apart, we grew up very close to each other.

My mom and dad had both been married before they married and had children as a result of those marriages. It became a yours, mine and ours type of family but we were all close and never felt divided by our sir names. As a matter of fact, we were one big happy family and we all considered each other as brothers and sisters and the half never entered into our definition of our relationships as siblings.

Our parents raised us to be one happy family and to never look at each other as not brothers and sisters regardless of our name. My older brothers and sisters treated Tom and me no different than they treated each other. And Tom and I held the same beliefs concerning them. As we grew older and were aware of the family situation, it changed nothing in the way we lived together or our regard for our older siblings. We were one big happy family and we irritated each other, played pranks on each other, got angry with each other and laughed together with each other in the same way other families have done.

But Tom and I were a pair, the younger brothers who were the babies of the family. Our older brothers and sister took care of us when they were old enough to do so.

But Tom was the baby and that could not be denied. My dad wanted to name him George but my mom said no way.

He then moved on to Pete and my mother was more against that than she was against George. Can you imagine what the poor kid would have had to live through with a name like Pete Petitt (pronounced Petite as in small). The kids in elementary school would have had a blast teasing him and he would have been in his share of fights. So, they agreed on Thomas with his middle name after my dad's father, Clarence. So, it was Thomas Clarence Petitt.

My earliest memories of Tom were when I was about four years old. We were living in a once active coal mining town by the name of Iselin which was located in Western Pennsylvania. We lived in an old company house which had been used to house miners when the mining operation had been active. The houses were not the best built homes and had been erected in a hurry in order to accommodate the many mine workers who were employed by the mine. These houses were drafty and cold in the winter and we weren't a family of wealth. My dad worked as a miner himself in a mine located elsewhere. He worked and my mother stayed home to care for us until he was laid off when the mine shut down. He then took a job working for one of our uncles on his trash truck and things were really tight.

Tom and I would play outside and, in the area close to the house. Times were much different then. There wasn't any worrying about a child being snatched away by some pervert. I don't remember much at all about Tom from when we lived in Iselin. I do remember the man who lived next to us was building a boat in his basement and Tom and I would go over there and watch. I also remember our dad taking Tom and me out back and sitting us on a bench and cutting up a piece of fruit for us with his pocket knife. Tom and I would sit and eat the fruit but to this day, I can't remember what kind of fruit it was. But I do remember it tasted good.

Another thing I remember about living in Iselin was when my dad would take Tom and me down the street to the home of an elderly Black man by the name of John Marshal. Now, I make a note of the mention that this man was Black because this was the mid-1950s and white people didn't normally socialize with the Blacks.

But my dad taught us that the color of a man's skin had no bearing on who he was or his character. So, we would sit on the porch of this man's house and listen as our dad and John Marshal talked. Our oldest brother, Link, cleaned John Marshal's house for him.

There was another elderly Black man who lived on the top floor of this house and his name was Albert. When our dad would take us down to John's house, Albert would always come down and join in the conversation. Back then, there was a donut truck, much like a lunch wagon or small food truck today, that would come down that old red dog (a type of coal cinder) street and Albert would stop him and buy a donut for me and one for Tom. Tom and I always remembered those times sitting on John Marshal's porch eating a donut and listening to those three men talk.

Tom was always a magnet for strays and in Iselin it was stray dogs. He was about three years old and he would go down the street a little way and when he returned, there would be a dog following him. If allowed, Tom would have had a regular ASPCA dog pound at our home. But our mom or dad would always shew the dog away and sent it back home. This was a trait which would be with Tom throughout his life. He sure did love those strays.

Our mother and father landed jobs working for a state hospital and with the increase in income, they were able to move us out of the company town of Iselin and to the community of Elders Ridge. It was located a few miles further up the road and we lived there for a brief time but I don't want to get ahead of myself. There are two events which stand out in my memory concerning Tom and me in the house at Elders Ridge.

There was a bathroom right off of the living room and Tom and I were playing in there one evening while our mom and dad were watching TV. We were close to the doorway and Tom fell backwards and landed against the baseboard which had a nail protruding out. He began to cry and our dad responded.

He got up and came into the bathroom and asked Tom what he was crying about and he told my dad that I had pushed him down on that nail. I hadn't touched him and I was shocked, even at that early age, that he would tell my dad this lie. I pleaded my case but it was no use.

The judge and the jury, my dad, had believe the testimony of my brother and my dad rendered my punishment. Now, we were both crying and making noise. I guess it's true, we don't have to learn to lie, we are born with that ability. That was it for play time that evening.

I got my revenge though. Tom and I shared a bedroom with a porch roof outside our bedroom window. Our dad had worked the graveyard shift and had been in bed a short time but Tom and I had been up early on this morning. We were playing and messing around like normal 4 and 5 years old do. We were both still in our whitey tighty underwear and one of us got the bright idea of going out onto the porch roof in our underwear. I don't remember how we decided Tom would go first but he did. I could have convinced him to go but I honestly don't remember.

So, we opened the window and Tom went out on the roof and when he was securely in place, I closed the window and locked it so he couldn't get in. I was jumping up and down and laughing at him and he was getting very angry. It was about nine in the morning and there was a fair amount of traffic. Finally, Tom had enough and he decided the only way to get back inside was to break the window glass. Now, window glass back then wasn't the double or triple pane glass we see today and when he hit it with his fist, it shattered. He came back inside and was really upset. He didn't like being stuck out there on the roof in his underwear.

We never gave it a thought that the roof covered a sunporch which was very high above the ground. If he had thrown a serious tantrum and wondered close the edge and fell, it would have probably killed him. Our dad couldn't have been asleep yet because the next thing we knew he was standing in our bedroom demanding to know what we were doing. Then he saw the broken window and the rest is a blur. When we were older, Tom thought it was he who locked me out on the roof and I would tell him he was wrong. Finally, our sister confirmed it was Tom who was stuck out on the roof in his underwear.

I started school when we lived in Elders Ridge and the school was located in Iselin. Most kids who attended there were from low-income families. I do remember that there was a small church building located next to the school building and once a week we would go into the church for a Bible class. That won't happen today.

One day I was outside during a recess period and heard fire trucks coming up the road. I watched as they raced past the school traveling in the direction of Elders Ridge. At that moment, a thought ran through my mind. "My house is on fire." Later I would find out that our house had burned.

I always wondered why that thought would have been in my mind. It could have just been the fear of a young boy seeing fire trucks racing in the direction of his house but it always seemed more than that to me.

Tom was about three or four years old at the time and my older brother Denny was at home with him that day. My mom and dad and had worked a graveyard shift and hadn't been home that long when the fire started. The house had a coal furnace and my dad had stoked it when he got home. What wasn't known was there was a crack in the flu or chimney and after he stoked it, the heat from the fire started the fire in an upstairs bedroom closet. It was the closet in my parent's bedroom. My mother had changed out of her work uniform and had just put on her housecoat when she saw the closet was on fire.

The house was old and went quickly. My mom and dad got out and Denny grabbed Tom and got him out. Tom didn't even have shoes on his feet. Denny was only concerned with getting Tom and himself out of the house. Denny was home from school that day for one reason or another but it was a good thing he was. My mom and dad were grabbing what they could and got out. My mom said she sat in the car and watched the house burn and cried. Everything they had worked so hard for in bringing this family together went up in the fire that day.

Now they had to start over from scratch. There wasn't renter's insurance and even if there was back then, they would not have been able to afford it. Everything was gone and what we had on our backs was all we had. We were placed with relatives in their homes when they volunteered to help. People donated items such as furniture, clothes and other stuff. There were nine of us in that family and we were spread out around Indiana PA with my mother's family. My sister Myra and I were staying with our Uncle Francis and Aunt Ada.

He was a Wesleyan preacher and they would drag us around Indiana County on Sundays and Wednesdays to the different churches where he would preach. We stayed with them because they lived in Iselin right across from the school where Myra and I attended.

I'm pretty sure Tom stayed with my mom and dad and with who they were staying. My mom and dad had to now find a place for us to live.

Eventually, they found a house just outside of Indiana and not far from our Uncle Link's church where we attended. It was across the road from the school Myra and I would be attending. But that wasn't the main reason they chose that house. It was the cheapest they could find on short notice and the condition of it was proof. It was in bad shape but at least we were together again and I was glad to get away from Aunt Ada. She was always trying to cut my hair off and Myra would tell her that our mom would not like that. Aunt Ada insisted it at least needed a trim. She said something to the effect that I looked like a shaggy dog. She then trimmed it but did not cut it all off. She used a pair of those old manual hair cutters.

It was also tiring being dragged around Indiana County on Wednesday evenings. I would go from a sitting position on the pew to a lying position as I fell asleep. That was not permissible. Aunt Ada would wake me and tell me it was not right to sleep in church. I was six years old; what did I know and I was tired. Never thought that was right when I was older and thought about it. I should have been home in bed getting my rest for school the next day.

Finally, and after a few months in that shack we were living in, we moved. Tom and I were in our glory. We were moving to a farm outside of Brush Valley and would be there for the next five years. Those were some of the best years of our childhood.

The Farm

In the early summer of 1957, our mom and dad moved us to a farm which was located about four or five miles outside of Brush Valley PA. They rented the farmhouse from a man named Paul Overdorf who was an insurance man in Indiana. His brother, Virgil, lived about a ¼ of a mile down the road and had his own farm. But Virgil farmed the property his brother owned and also had some cows on the property where we lived. I was about six and Tom was about four when we moved out there. There were wide open spaces and we could run and make all the noise we wanted to. Virgil Overdorf was a really nice man and helped Tom and me get comfortable around the cows. We had never seen an animal that big in our lives.

We would play in the barn up in the hay lofts and check out all the farm equipment in there. This was a whole new world for us and we were having a blast. Our mom and dad had bought us some little cars and trucks which were similar to what is known as Matchbox cars today. Tom and I would play with those cars and trucks in the dirt behind the house. When it was warm, we would be out there all day playing with those little vehicles with our imaginations running wild. We would pretend we were adults going about adult business. And, sometimes we even pretended we were adults we knew and would pretend we were going to work, to the store, to the drive-in movies and anything else we could think of.

We went out in the morning and claimed which toy car we wanted and would play with it all day. We made roads in the dirt and even had places we would pretend to go and made a place in the dirt which represented it. That was one of our favorite pastimes. If we weren't doing that, there were other things that kept us busy like exploring in the barn or watching the cows.

Virgil taught us how to approach a cow and how not to get stepped on by a cow. Tom and I used to like tapping on the forehead of the cows because it was so hard. The cows were mellow and never reacted in a rough or mean way. But Virgil also taught us to stay away from the electric fence which kept the cows in. Well, I learned my first lesson in electrical conduits while I was checking out that fence. It was an early electrical engineering lesson when I touched it with a stick. I immediately learned that wet wood is a good conductor of electricity. Tom was much smarter than I was on that day. He stood and watched as I was jolted off of my feet and onto my backside. I was alright but I learned the hard way to not touch that electrified barbed wire with anything. Of course, Tom also learned from my ignorance that day and knew not to touch that fence.

As you pulled into the driveway of this home, the driveway continued onto a tractor trail which led to an old apple orchard about ½ of a mile up past an open field. Tom and I would walk up there a lot and check out the apples. We told our mom and she wanted to see for herself. So, we went up to the orchard and she found a tree which had huge apples on it. She picked a lot of them and went back to the house and made pies, dumplings and apple sauce out of them. We were so spoiled and didn't even realize it back then. If we saw our mom walking toward the apple orchard during apple season, we knew she would be making some apple goodies and we loved them.

On that property there was also a cherry tree, a pear tree, a peach tree, strawberries, raspberries and elderberries. Tom and I didn't care much for the elderberries but we ate everything else. There were also apples trees in the area around the house. We just never knew how good we had it with all that fruit surrounding us.

Speaking of berries, Tom and I took a walk after supper one evening. We walked up toward the orchard and turned around before we got there and instead of walking back down the trail, we walked in the tall grass next to the trail. We came across some red berries we had not seen before. So, we ate some but they had no taste so we kept going back toward the house. When we got back to the house, it was getting dark, so we went in. Our mom was in the kitchen. Entering the rear of the house brought you through a sun porch and then into the kitchen.

She asked us where we were and we told her but we made the mistake of telling her about the berries. Right away, she swung into mother mode and wanted to know what kind of berries they were. We told her they were red berries. That wasn't good enough. She wanted us to give her a full description of these berries. We told her they were small and round and had no taste. That did it; she began to mix some stuff up in two glasses of water. We asked her what it was and she told us we were going to drink it and it would make us vomit. She said it was Epsom salts and neither Tom or I liked the sound of that so we began to really plead our case but it was no use. She insisted we would drink it if we had to sit there all night.

By this time, we were both bawling our eyes out and telling her we weren't going to drink it. She wasn't budging and began to give us a lecture on poison berries and how she couldn't know if these berries were poison or not. So, we would drink the solution and vomit these berries up before they could poison us. Tom and I never ate anything we came across again unless we knew what it was. It was another lesson learned about farm life and country living.

Of course, living in the wide-open spaces gave us more freedom and also allowed us to get into more trouble. My dad loved dogs and always had at least one or two running around. One of the dogs had puppies and Tom and I just loved little puppies. One day, Tom and I got the litter of puppies, about seven or eight, and took them with us to the barn to play with them. We took them up into a hayloft and were playing around and then went back to the house to eat supper. My dad went out to feed the dogs and he came back in wanting to know where the puppies were.

Tom and I looked at each other and knew right away we were in trouble. We had left the puppies in the hayloft in the barn. It was getting dark outside and already dark inside the barn. We told our dad what we had done and that we forgot about the puppies when we came in to eat. He grabbed a flashlight and told us to go with him. He wanted us to show him where those puppies were so he could get them back to their mother. We got to the barn and climbed up in the hayloft and heard the puppies crying. My dad told us to get them down so, we grabbed them and made sure we had all of them and headed back to the shed where the mother was located. Needless to say, we received a strong lecture on not messing with the puppies again.

Well, we thought we got off pretty easy with that one. We didn't know that the pups couldn't be away from the mother when they were that young so we learned a lesson. We didn't mess with those pups after that.

Then, there was the time we almost burned down an old chicken coop. Myra used to like to get me and Tom to play dumb girl stuff. So, we thought we could clean the old chicken coop up a little since she wanted us to play tea party or something like that. Now, cleaning up the place wasn't what got us into trouble. It was the playing with matches. Tom and I were inside the old building with a pack of matches and we started lighting them. The next thing we knew, one of those matches fell and ignited some old trash. I was scared and ran but Tom was yelling fire and trying to get help. I thought I was really in big trouble and that's why I ran. I was more afraid of the trouble I would be in than the fire.

Fortunately, Tom told Vonnie who was in charge while our mom and dad were at work and they got the fire out. It wasn't really a big fire and was easy for them to put out but we were still in trouble. Speaking of matches, there was the Sunday morning when Tom and I got up before everyone else. I ask Tom if he wanted to try smoking a cigarette and he said yes. I knew where Denny kept his cigarettes and we got a pack and went down behind the old chicken coop. I lit one and took a big drag of it and then handed it to Tom. He did the same and then I began feeling dizzy and nauseated. Tom handed it back to me and I told him I didn't want anymore and he said the same. We put the cigarette out and vowed to never touch one again. It was a Lucky Strike non-filter. We were both dizzy and our stomachs felt really bad. We didn't get caught doing that one but we sure paid the price for it.

My mom and dad had worked a graveyard shift and were in bed sleeping. Tom and I had watched our dad chop fire wood with an ax so we thought we would give it a try. Now, it was a chore to lift the ax and swing it. But I thought I could do it. So, we went into the basement, found the ax and went out back to chop some firewood. I took a few swings with the ax and it wasn't as easy as it looked when my dad did it. Then I took a big swing and missed the wood and the ax went through the side of my shoe and cut my little toe. I thought for sure I had cut my toe off and was screaming. Tom grabbed me and helped back to the house.

We went upstairs and into my parent's bedroom. My mom heard the door open and me crying and knew right away we had got ourselves into trouble again. She sat up and swung her legs over the side of the bed and asked, "What's going on? What did you two get into now?" Tom was telling her in a very excited voice, "Bill cut his little toe off with an ax!" Of course, my mother's next question was, "An ax? What were you two doing with an ax?" Tom told her, "We were chopping wood for dad."

My mom took my shoe off and my bloody sock and took me to the bathroom and cleaned it up and said, "You didn't cut your toe off. You cut it but it's not that bad." When she said 'not that bad' I was happy and asked, "So, it doesn't need stitches?" She said it wouldn't and I was a happy boy but we still received another lecture on using tools which are dangerous. My mom was really upset and Tom and I thought for sure we were in trouble again but she wasn't going to smack us when both of us had a terrible scare. And, we woke her up. That's like getting woke up in the middle of the night when you have to go to work in the morning.

Okay, don't play with matches, don't mess with the puppies and don't use our dad's dangerous tools. Were we learning? You would think so but we were two curious boys younger than ten years old. Tom had a habit of going outside without shoes on. So, early one morning, he and I went outside and were walking toward the old chicken coop when I heard Tom screaming. He had stepped on a broken piece of glass. He had cut his instep and was bleeding a lot. So, I put him on my back and carried him upstairs into our parent's bedroom. Here we go again. They were both asleep when I barged in with Tom on my back and again, my mom heard the door open and Tom crying. It was the same routine. She checked Tom's foot and decided he needed stitches. She cleaned his foot and then she got dressed and took him to Homer City to see Doc Hanna. He stitched up Tom's foot and when they returned, it was lecture time again. But this time it was directed mostly at Tom since he had been told by our mom about going outside without shoes on. But I wasn't off of the hook. She told me, "You should know better when he does that. You need to make him get shoes on when you two go outside. It was beginning to seem like Tom and I were always getting hurt in some way that always disturbed our parent's sleep habits. But I do believe that was the last time we had to wake them over an injury.

One day during the summer months, Tom and I had been inside and when we went back out, I was chasing him into the area behind the house where there was a tree. It was the same area where we built roads and played with our little cars. Tom climbed up that tree and moved out onto a limb which was a little too weak to hold him. It happened so fast that I couldn't believe what was happening. That limb snapped and came crashing down before either of us could think.

When Tom landed on the ground, his left wrist was bent back beneath him. It was broken and he started to cry. I ran into the house and got our mom and she came running out to see what happened. She knew right away it was broken and off they went to see Doc Hanna. When they came home, Tom had a cast on his arm and was telling me all about how the doctor had fixed it. I asked him, "Did it hurt when he fixed it?" He answered, "No, he gave me something that made me feel like I was under water or something." That didn't make sense to me and our mom said, "The doctor gave him a sedative and he was groggy but felt no pain."

Tom was proud of that cast on his arm and kind of liked it until it his arm started to itch and he couldn't scratch it. So, our mom gave him a wire clothes hanger (which was the only kind back then) so he could slide it down inside the cast and scratch. But after six weeks of that cast, he was ready to have it off. He was only about six or seven years old when this happened and a country doctor setting it proved to become a bigger problem for him a few years later. But I don't want to get ahead of the story.

Since both of our parents had to work to support the family, Vonnie was the oldest daughter and was always in charge when our mom and dad were at work. Link married soon after we moved to the farm and Denny was never home so the chore of attempting to keep me and Tom in line was given to Vonnic. It would be an understatement to say we drove her crazy. I have never denied the fact that Tom and I were two little hellions. We were brats and more than a handful for any older sister. During the summer months when it was nice outside, Tom and I would be outside all day and Vonnie didn't have to be concerned with us making a mess, tearing up the house and making trouble for her. She made sure we got breakfast and lunch and dinner depending on what shift our parents were working.

If they were working an afternoon shift, she would fight to get us inside when it started to get dark.

Following a few healthy threats, we would go in and then she had to get us upstairs for a bath. That was another headache for her. But eventually, we got our bath and then it was downstairs and watch TV. It wasn't as smooth of an operation as I have made it sound here and my sister can attest to that fact.

Our dad had a son, Virgil, to his first wife and he came to live with us shortly before the fire in Elders Ridge. When we lived on the farm, one of Virgil's chores was to sweep the kitchen floor and keep it clean. Our mom had a few throw rugs in the kitchen and Virgil would have to pick these up, take them outside and shake any dirt out of them. Tom reminded me of how we used to torment Virgil when he was trying to pick those rugs up. He said we would jump on the one he was trying to pick up. So, when he moved to another, one of us would jump on that one. We thought it was funny until Virgil started to get really angry with us and then we would move on and let him do his job. Yes, we were brats and troublemakers. I had forgot all about that stunt until Tom reminded me. When he told me, I couldn't believe we did that. So, in my older years, even I thought that was wrong.

Tom had a creative mind and knew how to keep himself entertained. In the evening, when we were all watching TV, Tom would take a belt and two gloves and play cowboys out in the kitchen. The belt was a horse and the gloves were people. He would play like that for hours if you allowed him. One night while we were watching TV and during a commercial, I heard him playing with a belt and the gloves and went to agitate him. Although it was a very creative way to entertain himself while we were all watching TV, I thought it was kind of goofy and began to ask him what he was doing. He told me and I started to tell him how dumb that was (I was only wanting to irritate him) when my mom jumped in and said, "You let him alone. He's playing and not bothering anyone. Now get away from him and let him alone."

She was right, he was having a great time in his fantasy world of playing cowboy with a belt for a horse and two gloves for the cowboys.

He would take the gloves and pretend they were two guys fighting. He would slap the gloves back and forth against each other simulating a fight. I have to give him credit for being so resourceful. I'm not sure I could have ever come up with that idea. But that was Tom. He was always able to keep himself entertained.

During the summer months, Tom and I would stay up and watch TV after everyone went to bed. Denny was always out somewhere chasing girls or doing who knows what. He would come in late and Tom and I would be on the sofa watching TV and he would demand we get off so he could lie down. If we told him no, he would simply drag us off and put us on the floor. After he had done that a few times, Tom and I decided we were tired of it. So, we told our mom and she had a little talk with Denny. She came to us and told us, "I told Denny he's not allowed to drag you off of the sofa anymore when he comes in late. If he does it again, you let me know." She was gentle when she told us but we knew she had not been like that when she talked to Denny. He came in that night and said, "So, you little cry babies talked to mom about me dragging you off of the sofa." We told him that we were tired of him making us sit on the floor while he stretched out on the sofa. We also told him if he did it again, we would tell her again. He never did it again. We were the babies and knew we would always get our way when it was something like that.

Just a side note here: In all fairness to Denny, he wasn't always a nasty or a mean big brother. When he was home and not out chasing girls or whatever he did, he was good to me and Tom. I got on the bus one afternoon after school and my feet were like two blocks of ice. We had to wait outside the school for the bus to show up and it was really cold. I was hoping I could get on the bus and get the front seat right behind the driver but Denny was sitting there. So, I took the seat right behind him, hoping I could get some of the heat on my feet and get them warmed up. (high school picked up before us)

It wasn't working and I couldn't take it anymore and I started to cry. He heard me crying and wanted to know what I was crying about and I told him. He told me, "Get up here and you sit next to the window and stick your feet up to that heater. We'll ride the bus all the way around the loop so your feet can get warm." The heater was on the floor and I stuck my feet right up to it.

Virgil, our neighbor, was the bus driver and he had it going full blast. We could either get off of the bus at Virgil's house and walk about a ¼ of a mile up the road to our house or ride the bus all the way around a loop that came back right past our house. By the time we arrived at our house, my feet were warm. And, it was Denny who got Tom out of the burning house in Elders Ridge. No shoes but got him out.

Tom and I attended Brush Valley Elementary School in Brush Valley. It was a nice little country school where most kids were from families who lived in that rural area. It was known as living out in the country. We were from all walks of life and various income levels. The majority of us were on the lower income level. But I remember the kids as not ever looking down on anyone who they would have considered to be 'poor.' We didn't have much as a family but we always had food on the table and a roof over our heads. We had clothes that were not rags and we were always taken care of. Tom and I loved going to school in Brush Valley.

I remember a time at that school when I was in fourth or fifth grade and went into the boy's room. Tom was in there with another boy who was trying to pick a fight with Tom. Tom was ignoring him. The kid was from an upper grade level from Tom and I guess he was trying to bully him. I noticed Tom had not said anything or done anything so I told this kid to back off and stop picking on my brother. As I said this, he was standing in front of one of those urinals that went down to the floor level and I pushed him right into that urinal. The kid got out of the urinal and quickly left the boy's room. Tom just looked at me and said, "Why did you do that? I could have taken him."

But Tom and I weren't the type who would get involved with fighting. We didn't really have to worry too much about that at that school. It seemed that everyone got along and if they didn't, they stayed away. I don't remember ever knowing anyone at that school who I couldn't get along with and I don't remember Tom getting into any fights there. Young boys are always going to end up in a fight sooner or later but it didn't happen there.

The school was divided between grade levels 1-3 and 4-6. The lower grades were located on one end of the building with their area for outside recess time on that end.

The upper grade levels were on the other end with their outside area on that end. So, during a school day and once I reached the fourth grade, I never saw Tom at school unless we saw each other in the boy's room.

Tom started school at Brush Valley when I was in the second grade or maybe the third grade. Either way, he had a teacher, Mrs. Sayers, who probably should have retired years earlier. When I told the kids my little brother was in the first grade, they just looked at me and said, "Oh boy, do we feel sorry for him.

He has Mrs. Sayers for a teacher and she is really mean. She yells and screams at the kids and she's even scary to look at." Well, they weren't lying about her. Tom always complained about the way she screamed at them and was mean. She lived along the road that came out of Brush Valley on the way to where we lived. The blinds were always pulled down and the kids would tell stories about how creepy she was and how she didn't want anyone being able to see into her house. They told stories about never seeing her husband or about how she kept him locked away in there and tortured him. The stories were wild and crazy about Mrs. Sayers. Every time we drove past her house at night, me and Tom would just look at each. One time, Tom told our mom about all the stories he had heard about Mrs. Sayers but she told him it was simply rumors and stories not to be believed. We always remember Mrs. Sayers, the mean first grade teacher at Brush Valley. I never had her since I started school at Brush Valley in the second grade. The other kids used to tell me how lucky I was not to have had her for a teacher.

More From the Farm

Tom and I were about twenty-two months apart in age but our mom had many people thinking we were twins. When we were young boys, she would always dress us alike. We had the same shirt, same pants and same shoes. Maybe she was finding deals where it was two for the price of one. I don't know and really don't think that was it. I think she just enjoyed having us look the same and everyone thought we were twins. Eventually, we reached an age where we began to not want the look a like clothes anymore and began to have our own tastes.

When we lived on the farm, Saturday was the day our parents went shopping and that meant a trip to Indiana. Back then, there was no Walmart or shopping malls. It was all on main street in each town and that included Indiana PA. The Murphy's five and dime was across from the McCrory's five and dime and down the street was Montgomery Ward department store and a whole bunch of other small stores and businesses along main street which was actually named, Philadelphia Street.

After our mom hit the five and dime stores for what she needed, sometimes she would walk down to Montgomery Ward and try on dresses. She couldn't afford a new dress but she enjoyed trying them on. The women's department was on the second floor which overlooked about half of the first floor. She would go upstairs and try on dresses while Tom and I waited downstairs with our dad. There was a railing on the second floor and she would try on a dress and come over to the railing so we could see her in the new dress she couldn't afford to buy. Tom and I couldn't figure out why she would try on all these dresses and never buy one. As I got older and understood more, I realized what she had been doing.

But Tom and I would still be fidgety and our dad would have to settle us and tell us she would be done soon. And, it never failed, when she would finally come down without a new dress, Tom and I would want to know why she tried them all on and didn't buy one. How hard it must have been for her to try to tell us she couldn't afford one. Actually, I don't quite remember what she told us but I'm sure it was difficult to explain the situation. But years later, Tom and I both knew and understood why she tried on all those dresses while our dad waited patiently with his two rambunctious sons. It was a way of her feeling good by just trying the dresses on.

Following all of that was a trip to the grocery store. Mom and dad would go in the store and we waited in the car. We didn't understand then but knew later when we had kids of our own why we waited in the car. There were times when we were allowed to go in but not that often. When we were older that changed. Occasionally, our mom would buy a half gallon of ice cream. It came in a box like container and when we got home and everything was put away, she would slice the ice cream like it was a loaf of bread and we each got a slice. It was gone in one setting but we sure did enjoy it.

Tom's birthday was at the end of September and mine is in the first week in December. But our parents couldn't just buy for one on either birthday. I don't remember if Tom and I made a fuss when the other got presents on his birthday or if our parents did it to keep us both happy. Many times, it was the same thing or toy or game or whatever. It was the same at Christmas; if one got a certain toy, the other got the same toy. It prevented us from using each other's toy or fighting over them. Call it preventive parenting but it worked. We would always get similar type of gifts on birthdays and Christmas. But for the most part, we didn't fight too much over gifts and presents, that I can remember. I not going to say it never happened.

I remember the year that dad bought Tom and I first baseman gloves. Christmas afternoon Tom and I were outside with dad playing catch in thirty-degree temperatures. It didn't last too long but we had to do it. And besides, dad hardly ever did that regardless of the weather. There were Christmases when they bought us footballs and even a basketball, I think. Dad had played a lot of sports when he was younger. He was on a high school soccer team which had won a state title. He also played baseball as a catcher. He tried to convince me to play that position but I wasn't buying it.

I had begun to gain a real interest in sports but Tom wasn't all that interested while we were living on the farm. Tom could be by himself and keep himself entertained for hours as I explained earlier. He was also a story teller. What I mean is he could fabricate some good ones. Likc the dead cow story he told our mom and me one afternoon.

Tom had been outside and he came into the kitchen and told me and our mom he had seen a dead cow. She knew the only cows around there were Virgil Overdorf's cows so she told Tom to show her the dead cow. Tom led us all over that farm that day but we never saw a dead cow. We ended up in a field below the house and our mom finally told him, "Tommy, I don't think you really saw a dead cow. We have walked all around this farm and haven't seen anything like a dead cow. Let's go back to the house." But even in his later years, Tom swore he had seen some kind of dead animal. I suggested it might have been a deer and he agreed but we never saw it. That was an adventure neither of us ever forgot.

One of my most memorable times was when our dad got Tom and me out of school one afternoon to go with him to get our car out of the shop. It was late October or early November. I remember the leaves had all turn orange and brown and red but where still on the trees. It was a bright and sunny day and cool. Neither Tom or I knew anything about this but our dad showed up at the school and we were released. We couldn't figure out what was going on and when we got into the loaner car the dealership had given us, our dad explained. Tom and I always remembered that day not just because we got out of school early but because we got to go with our dad to get our car at the dealership. The dealer was in Turtle Creek which was close to Pittsburgh so it was about an hour's drive. Maybe you just had to be there but it was a great day for Tom and me.

Dad was kind of funny in a lot of ways. He bought his cars at the same place and bought gas for the cars at the same place and it didn't matter where we lived, he continued to shop at those places. I'm sure he bought gas at the Sunoco station in Clarksburg PA because it was closest when we lived in Iselin. He had an account there which he would pay off every month. It was the same with the buying a new car. It was always the same Chevrolet dealership in Turtle Creek, PA which is just outside of Pittsburgh. Some would say he was a dedicated customer of these places.

Winter was always fun for us at the farm. We were located at the highest elevation in the county and always got more snow than other places. In the late 1950s, snow removal on the roadways was not as efficient as it is might be today. So, when we got a snowstorm, and we had quite a few of them in those years, we were snowed in for a few days. Our mom and dad knew when a storm was coming and would always park the car down the road at Virgil Overdorf's barn because that road was always cleared before the road which went by our house was. That way, they could walk the quarter of a mile down to the car and be able to go to work.

It could be days before the road that went by our house was cleared and that meant if they stopped for groceries, they had to carry them up the hill to the house. That had to be brutal on them carrying bags of stuff while walking through deep snow. Sometimes, it meant going back down for a second load. The older kids would always get dressed and go to help. But when Tom and I would start to put on all of our winter garb, our mom would always stop us and tell us we were too little to help. Tom and I saw it as an adventure. We could have fun walking in all the snow and allow our imaginations to run wild.

We would imagine we were in a snow-covered wilderness somewhere fighting for our lives trying to reach safety. The only problem was that our mom was right. The bags of groceries were too heavy for us. But most of the time on the second trip, the older kids took a couple of sleds back down and pulled the stuff up on them.

Tom and I would go outside and build forts in the snow and play war but, when we were finished, building them seemed to be more fun than playing war. We did a lot of sled riding since there was a hill behind the house and across the road from the house. There seemed to be more than enough gloves for everyone and everyone had heavy coats and scarfs and boots and everything we needed to play in the snow. We would stay outside as long as we could and only came back into the house when our fingers and toes were like ice cycles and we couldn't take it any longer.

Tom and I would shed our coats and boots in the basement and bring our gloves upstairs to dry. We would park ourselves on a register to get warm and many times we were crying because our fingers were so cold it hurt. Our mom would say something like, "Alright, that's enough playing out in the snow today."

But about thirty minutes later, we were warm and ready to go again. Tom and I loved being outside regardless if it was in the snow or not. Sometimes we would go out just to be out in the snow. We would always find a way to keep ourselves entertained. There was the time when we found some old snow skis in the basement. It was just the skis with no way of attaching them to your boots so Tom and I got some old twine and rigged a way of tying them to our boots. Then, we went across the road and made a place to ski down the slight slope. There was a ditch at the bottom of the hill so, we filled it with snow and made a little jump out of it so we could get across the ditch. We piled snow in the ditch and packed it down and made it wide enough so we wouldn't miss it. It was stuff like that which kept us entertained.

Then there was the time when a storm hit and the car was at the house. The road was snow covered with about six to eight inches and our parents had to go to work that afternoon. They debated on whether to attempt to get out or not and finally decided to give it a try. It had been snowing hard all day and when they left, the snow was really piling up. They made this decision when they saw a state truck with a snowblower on it go by the house going in the direction of Virgil's farm. Our dad decided it would be safe to go at that time. But about twenty minutes after they left, our mom was back at the house. She told us they had only got down the road a little way when they saw the state truck at a stop.

The truck was stuck at a spot where the road went through a cut and there were about eight-to-ten-feet embankments on each side. The snow had blown over the road and was as high as the top of the embankments. That truck had been moving along without any trouble when it hit the wall of snow and was now at a standstill. Snowblowers were something new back then and we had never seen one before. I guess the driver thought he could 'blow' through anything. He was wrong and now dad was stuck behind him and neither vehicle could get out.

Right away, Tom and I made a beeline to the basement to get all our cold weather gear on and go check this out. Tom and I walked the short distance to where the car was stuck. It was weird because all we could see in front of the car was the big yellow state truck and snow all around it. Dad was shoveling around the rear tires trying to get a start when he tried backing up.

But it was no use. He always kept a small shovel and a few bags of coal cinders in the trunk during the winter months for a time like this. Tom and I were right there watching and finally he said, "Get out of the way. Go back to the house; you don't need to be out here getting in the way." We could tell he was getting frustrated but at that age, we didn't fully understand. I certainly do now. So, we backed off and just watched. The truck driver was sure he could back up if dad got the car out and I'm sure that frustrated him even more. He was probably feeling a little pressure.

One of the older kids was helping; I think it was Denny. They both worked at removing the snow and putting down cinders and finally, dad was able to get the car moving back. He kept going backwards until he got to the driveway and put the car in the driveway and then the truck was able to back away from the snow bank. The state truck went back around and was somehow able to make his way through that snow from the other side. To Tom and me, it was just another winter time adventure in the snow.

There was another time when dad was going to Clarksburg to fill the gas tank and Tom and Myra and I were with him. He had made a stop at the grocery store before he headed over to Clarksburg and bought a bag of potatoes and a bottle of pancake syrup. On the way to Clarksburg, dad always drove on the secondary road because it was the shortest distance. At one sharp curve in the road, the road was steeply banked and the car hit some ice and slid off of the road and into a shallow ditch. Dad got out and worked at trying to get out of the ditch but it was no use. Finally, he told us there was a farm close by and was going to see if the farmer could pull him out with a tractor. He left and we began to talk about how we were going to be stranded and lost and all we had to eat was raw potatoes and syrup. We went on and on with our fantasy and before we knew it, dad had returned with the farmer and a tractor.

The farmer and dad hooked a chain up to the car and the tractor pulled us out of the ditch without any problem. When we continued on to Clarksburg, we mentioned how we wouldn't have to survive on syrup and raw potatoes. But every time we traveled past that curve, Tom and I would remember how we were stuck there and the crazy idea of having to survive on raw potatoes and syrup.

The farmhouse had a coal furnace for heat and that was common in those days. On cold winter mornings, the house would be chilly.

Dad would go down and stoke the fire and the house would begin to warm up but Tom and I couldn't wait and we would be squatted on a register trying to get warm while mom cooked breakfast. She would be making us pancakes and telling us to get off of the registers. Mom would call us into thc kitchen to start eating and continue to make more pancakes. Tom and I would eat about six or eight pancakes each and mom just kept making them. When we finished eating, the house would be warm and then we would start thinking about going outside.

There was a thinking in the family that the house was haunted. Weird things would happen during the night like doors opening and closing, footsteps on the stairs and other weird things. But all this was heard when everyone was in bed and no one was downstairs to make these noises. Tom and I were scared to even go upstairs to bed some nights. We would be in bed and hear those footsteps on the stairs but no one was walking up or down the stairs.

We didn't do ourselves any favors either; we would watch a scary program on television before we went to bed and would just lie there wide awake and afraid of going to sleep. Mom would tell us not to watch that stuff and there were no ghosts or anything else in the house but us. That didn't work for Tom and me. And, on Saturday nights, we would stay up late and watch Chiller Theater with Chilly Billy Cardlilly (Bill Cardille). Back then it was all vampire and Frankenstein monster movies but it was really scary to us.

We would curl up in a blanket on each side of the fireplace and fall asleep watching. There were always two late movies and we would wake up when the second movie was on and be afraid to go up to bed. Sometimes we would wake up to find everyone else had went to bed and left me and Tom asleep on the floor. Hard to forget those Saturday nights and Chiller Theater.

Marbles and baseball cards were two of the items Tom and I used to collect. I think I was more of a baseball fan than Tom was but we both would get dad to buy us marbles. We would take them to school and shoot marble with the other kids and sometimes trade marbles. When we would shoot marbles, we would draw and circle in the dirt and take turns trying to shoot someone else's marble out of the circle. If you did that, you got to keep the marble you shot out of the circle. So, the key was to never play with marbles you really wanted to keep.

Tom and I would come home from school and compare our winnings. I always reminded him not to play with his favorite marbles. Of course, there were different kind of marbles. There were cat eyes, shooters, steelies and others which I can't remember. The steelies were nothing more than a ball bearing and kids would try to use them as a shooter because it was heavier and would easily knock a marble out of the circle. So, we made a rule that no steelies could be used as a shooter.

We used to bug dad to stop at the small store in Brush Valley so we could buy baseball cards. They were only a nickel (five cents) and there were five cards and a hard piece of flat bubble gum in the pack. The gum was always hard and stale but we didn't care and we would always look to see if we got a Pittsburgh Pirate player on one of the cards. I would look for a Pirate or a Yankee card and I saved them all for years. Tom was more into other stuff but it didn't matter. If one got baseball cards then both got baseball cards.

Sometimes we would take the cards to school and trade with other kids. I was pretty good at knowing the really good players and I could get some pretty good cards from the other kids. I would give Tom pointers on how to make good trades but he wasn't really all that interested. Tom was more interested in other ball games like square ball. Yeah, most people have never heard of it but Tom loved it. But I don't want to get ahead of the story and we'll come back to square ball later.

In the summer months, actually, the late summer months, Virgil Overdorf would be cutting hay and straw and bailing it up. When he was bailing straw which was the stubble left from when he harvested the wheat, Tom and I would wonder out to the field and ask if we could help. We could lift the bails of straw but not the hay. Virgil would entertain us and let us work with him and his sons for a while and then reach into his pocket and give us all his change and thank us for our help. Tom and I never did it for the money. We just wanted something to do and it looked like fun. We would toss the bails up on a wagon being pulled behind the tractor. Virgil's son, Denny, always helped us get the bails on the wagon. He could toss up two in the time it took me and Tom to throw up one.

The first time, we ran back to the house and told mom that Virgil gave us money for helping him. We thought that was really something. We had been paid for a job we did.

We really enjoyed it when Virgil got his old truck out in the field to load hay on. It was about a 1934 Ford flatbed and Tom and I thought it was really cool. Virgil's son Denny taught us how to drive the tractor but we were told to stay away from the truck. Tom and I enjoyed living on that farm and doing some of the stuff a farmer has to always do. But we just got a very small taste of what it takes to work a farm.

As with everything else Tom and I shared, we did the same with childhood diseases. I remember getting on the bus one morning and I felt terrible. I was really tired and felt nauseated. But I had to go to school and it wasn't long after classes started that the teacher called me out of the classroom and told me I was going to have to go home. She told me I had chicken pox and that my mother was on the way to get me. I knew something was wrong when I got up that morning but it was no use trying to tell someone I was sick because the older kids would have just thought I was trying to get out of going to school.

So, mom took me home and nursed me but it wasn't long before Tom also had the chicken pox. Now, mom was nursing both of us. Dad was working nights and Tom and I would sleep with mom. Tom was on one side and I was on the other and each of us were dealing with the itch of chicken pox. Our mother's favorite line during that time was, "Don't scratch the chicken pox." But the itch was really bad at times. She had some stuff she would put on them to ease the itching but it was still bad.

Then it was the mumps. We only had them on one side but it was hard for mom to keep us from jumping around which you're not suppose to do when you have the mumps. Two young and active boys who loved to run and jump and bounce around was a handful for mom and Vonnie when she was in charge. But the mumps were nothing compared to the chicken pox. And of course, Tom and I shared the mumps. We never had the measles but Myra did. Mom kept Myra closed up in her bedroom with the curtains drawn so it would stay dark. Tom and I didn't understand that and we would sneak upstairs and open her door and ask her why the room had to be dark. She would moan and tell us to go away and then mom would hear us and tell us get away from that room and get back downstairs.

And of course, there was always the flu. It was like clockwork that I would get the flu every year in the month of May. Mom would do her best to keep Tom away from me but he would eventually get it.

When Tom had the flu, it was mild compared to the way it attacked me. Tom would get it and a couple of days later be ready to go. But when I got it, it was like the Normandy invasion. It hit me hard and kept me down for close to a week sometimes. It clobbered me with everything it had; a high fever, nausea, cold symptoms and weakness. Now everybody will experience those but it felt like I got a double dose. But Tom would get a day or two after me and be up and around before I was. But mom would nurse both of us back to health. We were blessed to have a mother like her.

Leaving The Farm

The holidays and birthdays were always fun when we lived on the farm. Again, as a reminder, Tom and I were the babies in the family and we always got a little special treatment. As I have already mentioned, on our birthdays, we both received gifts. But depending on whose birthday it was, he got the better gift or more than one. But we understood and never made a fuss. But Christmas was different. We both got the same number of gifts and many times the gifts were the same. There would be one or two which were different and we never complained or fought over gifts that were different. And, mom and dad always bought us new socks and underwear which we didn't count as Christmas presents.

Our mom would decorate the house with all the Christmas decorations she had, and it seemed like she had enough to do two homes. We put the tree up about a week before Christmas but no one was allowed to help decorate it. Mom did that all by herself and didn't want anyone messing up her routine. But when it was finished, it was beautiful. Of course, dad was smart enough to know not to try to get involved. He yielded all the decorating to mom.

When she wasn't decorating the house, she was baking cookies and pies for Christmas. The Christmas day meal was always great. A big turkey and stuffing and everything to go with it. I remember one Christmas, it had snowed and then got very cold. There was about a foot of snow covering the yard and we lost power. Mom had bought ice cream for desert and was afraid it was going to melt. So, our oldest brother Link took it outside and buried it in the snow. We were ready for dessert and the ice cream was still hard and had not melted. Tom and I thought that was brilliant. We had pies and cookies well into the new year.

Thanksgiving was very similar to Christmas except for the presents. Mom made a big Thanksgiving meal for the whole family and the holiday atmosphere was easily felt in the house. Tom and I would go outside early in the day and find one way or another to entertain ourselves. It was a great time of the year. If the leaves had not yet been blown from the trees, they were all red, brown and orange type colors. We loved seeing the leaves change colors but we also loved dragging them into a big pile when they fell. We would pile up the leaves and then jump into them. I can still smell the odor of those dried leaves.

Sometimes we'd take a walk up past the barn and toward the old apple orchard. We both had pretty good imaginations and could fantasize about all kinds of different situations as we walked along. It's amazing how we didn't need a video game to create these fantasy worlds and situations for us. We could create with the best of them. Finally, we would hear someone calling for us and telling us it was time to eat. We would make a beeline back to house and take our seats at the big dining room table. That was Thanksgiving for Tom and me when we lived on the farm.

Halloween was another holiday Tom and I looked forward to. It had nothing to do with witches and goblins, it was all about the candy. There was no buying a costume at the store either. Again, creativity came into play for Halloween. We would get a mask at the store and that was all and you better keep it for as many years as possible because you might not get another for a while. So, Tom and I would dig into some old clothes and make ourselves to look like anything but ourselves.

Mom or dad would take Myra, Tom and me into Brush Valley and drop us off and designate a place to be for pick up and what time. Then we made our rounds through the small village of Brush Valley and always had more candy than we really needed by the time we were picked up. Then it was home and time to dig into the candy and begin stuffing our faces until it was taken away from us and told we had had enough. We didn't really care if our masks matched the way we were dressed and we never tried to compete with each other concerning our costumes. We simply enjoyed the fun of begging for candy as we went house to house. And, we didn't have to worry about fentanyl laced candy or razor blades in apples. It was a different time and a different world back then.

Easter Sunday was again all about the candy and the goodies. I don't remember Tom and I ever believing in an Easter Bunny hopping around bringing candy or whatever. We always knew it was mom and dad who provided the Easter baskets. When we were attending our Uncle Link's church, we would get the easter baskets before church but never allowed to eat any goodies from them. It was Sunday breakfast just as always. If mom and dad were working, which they had to do on some holidays, Vonnie made sure we ate breakfast first and goodies later.

Of course, there was always a big meal on Easter and lots of baked goods. Mom used to make her own Easter eggs. They were big and covered with chocolate. I couldn't even begin to say how she made them or the ingredients but they were really good. She made quite a few of them and they lasted for a while following the holiday.

Finally, July 4th was a holiday Tom and I always looked forward to. If mom and dad weren't working, we would go to the fairgrounds in Indiana PA. Mom always packed a big basket or cooler full of food. We would find a place on the slightly sloped hill in the grass which overlooked the race track. There were stock car races every year and we would sit there and watch the races and eat lunch. We would spend the day at the fairgrounds and we loved it. Again, it didn't require much to entertain us. There was always a traveling carnival there on the 4th and with it was a dunk tank. The guy everyone was trying to put in the water was really good at insulting people. It was his way of getting people to spend their money while trying to dunk him.

Tom and I could stand down for hours just listening to the guy picking on people while trying to get them angry at him and spend their money. He had some good lines and one I always remembered was when a guy with big ears would come by to watch. The guy in the dunk tank would call out to him and say, "Well, look at you. You look like a '59 Chrysler coming down the road with the back doors wide open." He had those kinds of lines for anyone who looked a little different and they worked. People were lining up to try to put him in the water. That was entertaining to me and Tom.

Some years, after the races, they would have pro wrestling matches but you had to have a seat inside where the bleachers were to see them and that cost money. Tom and I were too young to realize this was all choreographed and mostly fixed outcomes.

We would stand down where the wrestlers would cross from the dressing tent to the bleacher entrance and the ring and beg for autographs. Most of the guys ignored us but we were persistent and finally a guy by the name of Ace Freeman stopped and gave his autograph to me and Tom.

Following the matches was when the fireworks started. Tom and I were always back on the hill with mom and dad by that time. We would lie back in the grass and watch the fireworks light up the sky. They lasted for twenty minutes to half an hour and when they were over, it was time to pack up and head for home. It was always a big day for Tom and me and we always slept well that night.

Every summer while we were living on the farm, we attended a family reunion on our mother's side of the family. It was the Lentz family reunion and it was held somewhere in the Greensburg PA area at a park. This was a big event for Tom and I. Mom would always buy us new clothes for the event. I guess she wanted us to look nice for everyone else. Parents do that kind of stuff still today. The kids have to look good so others don't think you're neglecting them. I think she just wanted us to look presentable. We would wear clothes to play in during the day and after the evening meal, the adults would have a dance in a big pavilion. We would change into the new clothes for that. But that was our mom. She always wanted us to look good and I think most mothers are like that.

We would be playing with kids we were related to and never saw before and might have never seen again. There would usually be at least one fight break out over something. One year I got hit and the head with a rock and was knocked out cold. We were playing in what was like a dry creek bed and the kids starting arguing and fighting about something and the next thing I knew I was waking up in that big pavilion and my mom looking at me. Tom said he went after the kid who threw the rock and was going to tear into him but the other kids stopped him. Within minutes of when I came around, I was back out there playing with the other kids while my mother tried to keep Tom and me next to her. That didn't work.

Then, before we knew it, it was Labor Day and time to go back to school. Tom and I were not exactly fans of going back to school in September. Yes, September was when we went back to school, not the middle of August. But it didn't matter to us because we didn't want to go back.

As we finished the school year in 1962, our parents told us we were moving away from the farm. That didn't sit well with Tom and me. They decided it was too far to drive to work and it was really hard during the winter when we got those bad snow storms. So, they rented a house in Blairsville, Pa which was only about four or five miles from work instead of twenty or more.

Tom and I had grown so accustomed to having all that space to roam and make all the noise we wanted to make and now our parents were moving us into town. We simply hated the idea of just being in town. We left the farm in June of '62 and moved into Blairsville. The house was on the corner of Walnut and Brown streets and the yard was about the size of a hospital supply closet and some of that was taken up by bushes between the grass and the sidewalk. What were we supposed to do with that? That was in front and to the side and nothing in the back except another walkway and a house. We really didn't like this.

We got to know a couple of kids up the street. They had bikes and Tom and I didn't have bikes. They would allow us to ride them but one day I guess I had peddled to far and when I came back, I was told not to ask to barrow the bike again. They were brother and sister and mom and dad knew their parents from work. I remember their father would take the TV out on the front porch in the evenings and watch the Pirate game. I would go up and watch the game with him. Tom wasn't into baseball that much but didn't mind playing.

There was a big open space about two or three blocks from the house where we could play ball or whatever else we wanted to do there. But it was mostly playing baseball. Our first summer there, we had to really get serious about how to entertain ourselves. A lot of the time, we would just sit on the porch steps and watch the traffic go by. Walnut street was the main north/south street which ran through town so there was plenty of traffic on it all day long. For us, this was something different since we had lived on the farm for five years. We never saw a great deal of traffic go by the house and when a vehicle did go by, it was usually a neighbor.

That first summer wasn't much fun but things got a little better when school started and we were able to meet more kids and create more friendships. This is when Tom learned about square ball. All I ever knew about this game was it was played with a ball about the size of a volleyball or soccer ball.

There was a big square with four smaller squares inside the big square. Beyond that, I couldn't begin to tell you how to play the game but Tom loved it and the kids at the elementary school he attended played it all the time. The elementary school was about a block down the street from our house.

Tom would go down there with one of those balls and play all by himself for hours. I would go down and bounce a rubber ball off the brick wall and simulate a baseball game. But Tom was down there for hours bouncing that ball in a game of square ball all by himself. I think it was our first year in Blairsville that Tom went down to the school to play square ball by himself (I don't know how he did that). It was his birthday and mom had planned a small birthday get together for him with cake, ice cream and presents. But Tom wasn't there; he was down at the school playing square ball by himself. I had to go down and tell him to come home to celebrate his birthday. He said he had forgot all about it being his birthday. That's when we knew Tom was developing into an absent-minded air head. More on that later.

Another of our favorite past times was bouncing a tennis ball off of the side of the house. We would stand in the street and throw the ball up against the house. That worked pretty good until mom and dad were working the graveyard shift and had to sleep during the day. It was the same results we got when we lived on the farm and would jump off of the arms of the sofa onto the floor. It was like the whole house was rattling and mom would come down stairs with a belt in her hand. We stopped jumping off of the furniture when her and dad were sleeping during the day.

It was not quite the same with the ball bouncing off of the house but we did get the message when we woke mom or dad up. That's probably when we discovered it was easier to go down to the school and play ball. It was a brick building so it was easy to bounce any kind of ball off of it without disturbing anyone. We didn't have those problems when we lived on the farm. It was different; we just tried chopping off toes and burning down buildings and breaking bones. It still required mom getting up from her sleep but she was more compassionate.

Tom was able to make friends easily. He began to become friends with a lot of kids he attended school with. Of course, he learned to play some of the games they did like square ball.

But Blairsville was different than Brush Valley. Brush Valley was in a rural community and most kids live out of town on farms or just out of town. Blairsville was made up of people who worked for the railroad or the state hospital or at a factory which would close about two years after we moved there. There was no rural element except for the few kids who lived out of town and they, for the most part, attended a different school.

Tom and I had to learn fast how it was to live in town and get to know other kids in town. But as I mentioned earlier in the book, Tom had a thing for attracting strays and it was no different in Blairsville. I remember him dragging a guy home who was about fourteen years old and Tom was about nine. I don't remember how or why Tom got to know this kid but once he came back to the house with Tom, he was always coming to the house. His name was Blair Tunstel (unsure of the spelling) and he came from a very bad family situation. His dad was a drunk and didn't work and I don't remember if his mother was in the picture or not. His older brother, Clyde, had to provide for himself and Blair.

The whole situation was a mess and I felt bad for them and I know Tom did too. But Blair kept coming around and I was personally getting tired of him. Blair had a serious crush on a girl who lived down the street from us who was also fourteen and had a crush on me which mom put an immediate stop to. So, Blair would beg me to go talk to her about him. He would tell me how madly in love he was with her. I told him no and he had to go talk to her himself. The guy just bugged me and when he would come around, I would make myself scarce. Finally, mom had to tell Tom that Blair was too old to be hanging around with him. So, Blair stopped coming around and a few months later the girl down the street move away and that settled the problem.

Mom did feel bad for him and his family situation but she was right. A fourteen-year-old has no business hanging out with a nine-year-old. She just didn't know what kind of ideas Blair might put into Tom's head. Blair was a little immature and as I look back, I don't think Blair would have done that. I would soon discover that the kids who were Blair's age made fun of him and they wouldn't have anything to do with him. So, Tom did what he had always done with stray dogs no one wanted, he brought Blair home with him. That was Tom; he had a big heart and only wanted good for people he met.

Tom and I made it through our first winter in Blairsville but it was nothing like the winters on the farm. There was not much outdoor activity like there was on the farm. Tom attended the elementary school down the street and I attended the Jr./Sr high school about four or five blocks in the other direction. The school wasn't big enough for the Jr. and Sr. high school students to attend at the same time so Myra, who was in high school, would attend school at seven in the morning and then I, being in my first year of Jr. high, would attend at noon. I would sleep in until about ten and Myra had the whole afternoon available every day. Tom went to school at the normal time. A new school was eventually built and I was in the first freshmen class to attend.

The following spring, dad signed Tom and me up to play Little League baseball in town. It was too late to play the previous year when we moved to town. But the next year we were ready. Tryouts were held and Tom and I went through the drills and then it was time for the draft and to pick players. Years later when I managed Little League teams, it was just the managers who attended the draft and made their picks. In Blairsville, kids and parents could attend and the managers could talk to prospects before they began to draft players. So, dad took Tom and me to the draft and eventually the manager for the Kiwanis sponsored team came to talk to me and dad. He wanted me to be his catcher.

There was no way I was going to be a catcher. I was either a first baseman or an outfielder. He guaranteed me the team would finish first and I would be an all-star. But only if I agreed to be a catcher. I wasn't having it and dad, who had been a catcher, tried to talk me into it. I told him no. So, when the manager came back around, he asked if I had changed my mind and I told him no and he walked away. He didn't draft me or Tom. I was okay with that. But the team sponsored by the Elks Club drafted me and then Tom. Tom and I would be on the same team which has always been guaranteed by Little League.

That late Spring and early Summer, Tom and I and some other kids would go down the street to that clearing and play whiffle ball or pick up baseball. One day we were playing and a kid rode up on a bike and began to make fun of us. He told us were didn't know how to play and we were just a bunch of losers. We asked him if he wanted to play but he just continued to mock us.

He said he didn't want to play with kids who weren't good players. Tom and I were getting a little upset over his remarks about the way we played. I told him that Tom and I played on a Little League team in town and were good players. He told me we weren't good enough to play on a real team and then rode away. Tom and I were about ready to go at it with him but he left and we cooled off and went back to playing.

Tom and I had a game that evening and we were walking down to the field in uniform when that same kid rode up along side of us and began to apologize for the way he acted earlier. He said, "Wow, you guys really are on a team. You weren't kidding. Do you have a game now?" We told him we did and told him where the field was and he should come done and watch. He told us he was staying with his grandparents for a few weeks and didn't really know anyone. He was angry about having to stay with his grandparents and decided to pick on us just to vent. He apologized again and Tom and I told him to forget it. We never saw him again.

I only had one year to play on that team because of my age but Tom had two. When I moved up to Pony League the following year, he was still on the Elks team. As hard as I could hit the ball that year and always seemed to be on base, I never hit one over the fence, during a game. But the following year, Tom hit a home run. Tom would be the first to tell anyone he wasn't much of a baseball player but he was proud of the homer he hit and I reminded him he had done something I hadn't done the year before. That was the last year that Tom played baseball. He just didn't have the interest in that I did. But Tom had other talents.

In junior high, he played basketball and wasn't too bad. He shot the ball with two hands and was good at that. The coach tried to teach him to shoot with one hand but it wasn't working. I tried to teach him but no deal. So, I left him alone and let him shoot with two hands. It was a throwback way of shooting like the players did in the '20s and '30s. He would still play baseball in pick up games and if I got a new glove so did he. But in a few years, Tom would discover what sport he was really good at.

Moving Up to the Northside

In the summer of 1964, our parents bought a house on the northside of Blairsville. Everyone would split Blairsville into either the north side or the south side. When we moved to Blairsville and lived on Walnut Street, we were on the south side of town. All my friends lived on the north side and Tom's friends were mostly on the south side. But Tom and I never bought into the north-south thing. As far as we were concerned, people lived where they lived. There was no family income separation between the north and south. It was just an in-town rival of sorts that kids started.

Mom and dad wanted to get us into a home with a yard and some space to enjoy the outside. Route 22 ran between where our home was located and the main body of town. We liked that because we were actually out of town and weren't cramped by other houses so close. Our neighbor to the east of us had a big home with a large yard. He had wanted to buy the house which mom and dad bought but they got it first. He really seemed to hold a grudge over that. When we moved in, we were on his end of our front yard and he came over to introduce himself and then was very clear about keeping off of his property.

I was thirteen and Tom was eleven and we had no reason to wonder into his yard. There were some fruit trees which separated our property from his and the trees were on our side of the line. Tom and I immediately labeled him an old grouch. He was crystal clear about wanting the house for his grandson and being upset about not getting it. Our mom told us to never go on to his property and we told her that wasn't going to happen. There was a plumb tree at the property line and Tom and I would pick plumbs from it. If he saw us, he would watch us until we walked away.

After we had lived there for a while, he became a little more friendly but Tom and I didn't trust him. We never went into his yard and never gave him a reason to complain.

On the other side of us was the Frue family. There was Jack, his mom and her dad. Jack was about the same age as Tom or a year younger. There was a big open area behind their house and we used to play whiffle ball there. Of course, there was the time we were playing with a baseball and hit it through another neighbor's window. Our dad had to buy the glass and replace it. We received strict and stern instructions about never playing with a baseball out there again.

Mr. Frue, Jack's grandfather, used to sit in the basement next to the old coal furnace and tell us stories about the Negro League players. He would talk about Satchel Paige and Josh Gibson and Cool Pappa Bell and other players. Of course, there was a lot of embellishment and he really enjoyed telling us these stories. We would go home and ask our dad about these players and tell him what Mr. Frue had told us. He would always say, "Well, yes that did happen but not quite like that." I believe he also enjoyed the way Mr. Frue stretched the truth of the events when we told him.

Tom and I really enjoyed living on Dunne Ave. across the highway from town. We had plenty of space and weren't closed in but were still a short walk away from downtown. The only drawback was where our bedroom was located in the house. It was right over the garage and when mom and dad would work second shift, they got home a little after midnight. If they put the car in the garage, we would be awakened by the garage door opening and closing. It never failed. Sometimes, Tom would get up and go out to see mom and dad and mom would always say, "What are you doing up. Get back to bed. You have school tomorrow." And then Tom would tell them they woke him when they opened the garage door.

Christmas that year, our parents bought a reel-to-reel tape recorder. We had a blast with that thing but our parents were afraid we would break it or mess it up somehow. So, they kept it in their bedroom and told us we could only use it when they were home. Well, that was like telling glue not to stick. When our parents worked second shift, Tom and I would go into their room and use the recorder. We adlibbed all kinds of crazy stuff.

Before television became a fixture in homes and radio was still the way most people entertained themselves, there was a program called Amos 'n' Andy. It was a comedy series about two Black men who were actually played by two white guys. Later, it was a TV program and of course, the actors were Black. It was a very funny program. Tom and I only knew the TV program and we decided to do a parody of the show and changed the names of the characters. We simply adlibbed our way through about an hour every night. When we were finished, we would play it back and listen to it. Then we would erase it because we weren't supposed to be playing with it while our parents were at work.

One night, Tom and I did our little parody of Amos 'n' Andy and forgot to erase it. When we got home from school the next day, our parents were off and our mom asked if we'd been playing with the tape recorder. Tom and I looked at each other and knew we had been caught. Then mom said, "It's okay if you were. Your dad and I listened to what you two recorded and we haven't laughed that hard in a long time." Then, it was like relief. We weren't getting scolded for playing with the tape recorder. But there were also a few cuss words thrown in there and we thought for sure she was going to hammer us for that. So, I told her, "Wow, I thought you were going to get on us for using some swear words." She thought for a minute and said, "Well, it was really funny but you could have been just as funny without the language. No more of that!"

Soon after that, Tom and I tired of that routine and didn't do it anymore. We were both into music and loved listening to the radio when we could. It was all Top 40 format or Country back then and it was all on AM radio. The only music on FM was classical music. Tom and I listened to a radio station in Latrobe, PA, WQTW. It was a daylight only operation. It signed on at sunrise and signed off at sunset. That's the way it was licensed by the FCC. At night, we could pull in powerful radio stations out of New York City, Detroit, Chicago or Cleveland. They were the 50,000 watts AM transmitters.

We didn't really care about the technicalities just the music. We would use that tape recorder to record our favorite songs and then listen to them. I can remember coming home one day in March of 1966 and Tom telling me he was able to record a Mommas and the Poppas song we both liked. California Dreaming, I think it was. It was about this time Tom began his interest in guitar playing.

Our Uncle Jack, our mom's brother, was a really good guitar player and I think this stirred an interest in Tom. Uncle Jack would come to visit when we lived on the farm and he always brought his electric guitar and small amplifier with him. He and his first wife would sit at the kitchen table and talk with our mom and dad for a while and then we would always bug him to play his guitar for us. He would go out to his car and get it and set it up and begin to play. I can still hear it today. He was really good. Tom told me years later that Uncle Jack took lessons from a man who told him if he missed a chord, he would smack his fingers. He meant the guy would really smack them and cause pain. Uncle Jack told Tom he learned not to miss any chords.

Our Aunt Evelyn, our mom's sister, also played the guitar and was pretty good. She wasn't quite as good as her brother but still good. She had been working in some kind of plant where she operated a cutoff machine. It was the kind where you stick a piece of sheet metal under the blade and it slams down and cut the material. Well, she got three of her fingers in it and lost them. She and her husband were divorced and she was living alone. Our mom had her come and stay with us for a while. This was after our dad had died (more on that later). She brought her guitar with her and since she had lost the fingers on her right hand (she was righthanded), she could still play.

Her guitar was an acoustic type and she got it out one evening and was playing some stuff Tom and I didn't recognize. You could see the interest Tom had in wanting to learn how to play. Aunt Evy gave him the guitar and began to show him how it was done. Of Course, he had a long way to go since he had never had the opportunity to learn yet. Actually, while she was playing that night, Tom and I asked her to play something we listened to. She said she didn't know any of the songs we listened to. She was only familiar with barroom type Country stuff. So, I told her, "If I give you the lyrics and sing a little of it, can you pick it up?" She told me to go for it so there was a song which was popular at the time called, Let It All Hang Out by The Hombres. I gave her the lyrics and sang a little of it and she picked it right up and took off. She enjoyed it and we had a blast that night. Needless to say, Tom eventually had a guitar.

On the farm when I chased Tom up that tree and he fell and broke his wrist, it would become a problem for him as he got older. When he was about twelve years old, we were living on Dunne Ave.

As he grew and his bones grew with him, his left wrist, which had been broken when he was younger, did not grow right. I'm not a doctor so I don't know how to explain it but the wrist joint was deformed. I remember our mom telling us that when it was broken, his bones were still kind of soft. When the doctor set the broken wrist, the joint grew in a deformed manner. Or, something like that. Anyway, when he was about twelve years old, our mom took him to a Children's Hospital in Pittsburgh to have it rebroken and reset and the bone shaved.

It was in the Fall season of the year and Tom had a cast on his left arm from his hand up to his shoulder. Up the hill and behind our house was a housing community and there was a big open field up there where we would play football. There were a bunch of kids from up there and me and Tom and some others. There was Tom, with a full cast on his left arm playing football with us. It was touch football but I told him he wasn't allowed to hit anyone with that cast. I remember watching him run along the simulated sideline with the football and that big cast.

When we got home, our mom asked where we had been and what we were doing. Tom, not thinking, told her we had been playing football. She didn't like that response. She looked at him and said, "No more football with that cast on your arm. You can play when it comes off." Tom continued to plead his case but it was no use. That cast was on for six weeks and when he went back to have it removed, he was really disappointed because they replaced it with one which was only up to his elbow. So, as it turned out, he was on the shelf for about three months. He still did stuff he wasn't supposed to do and just hoped nothing would go wrong. He handled it very well. He handled it probably better than I ever would have. He had more patience than I did.

There was a man who lived on our side of town who had an apple tree in his backyard which had delicious apples. He had caught kids trying to sneak into his yard and take apples off of that tree. He would always catch them and was very mean and abusive about it. A few of my friends told me about this guy and we made it a point not to mess with him or his apple tree. One night after Tom and I came home from being out with our friends, he told me about him sneaking into this guy's yard. The guy caught him and they all started to run.

There was a fence across his yard and they all made it over the fence except Tom. He told me the guy hit him with some kind of club right on his head. The guy chased him to the fence and as Tom was climbing over it, the guy clubbed him. I told him he needed to tell our parents. I said, "This guy can chase you out of his yard, he can call the police but he can't hit you with a club over some apples." He didn't want to say anything because he thought he would be in trouble for stealing an apple off of this guy's tree. He was afraid mom would punish him and I told him, "What were you doing in that guy's yard anyway? Everyone knows that guy is crazy." Tom said he never heard anything about him and he refused to tell our parents what happened. But he never went back into the guy's yard again.

As I mentioned earlier about Tom and his strays, when we lived on Dunne Avenue, there was a boy who lived down the road a little way and he attached himself to Tom. Tom had not become friends with him or anything like that, he just decided he was going to be one of Tom's friends. His name was Bob Andrews and he lived with his stepmother and his stepsisters. His dad was a long-haul truck driver and was never around. His stepmom was really mean to him and he, being the only boy in the small house, was the odd ball. His stepsisters were mean to him also so Bob started to spend all his time at our house. Tom and I did feel really bad for him because of the way he was treated at home. He really didn't know his new family. His stepmom was a mean and cruel person and she even looked like the Wicked Witch of the West. The girls were no better. He was a boy who had been dumped on them and was disturbing their lives. Whatever that consisted of.

Bob irritated Tom sometimes. Tom didn't lose his patience very often but Bob could do it. Tom told me that even though he felt sorry for Bob, he did bug him sometimes. Bob would be at the house for hours and mom would eventually have to tell him it was time to go home. She knew he didn't want to go but it would be getting late in the evening and she had to send him home. Bob ate with us, watched TV with us and hung out at our house all the time. And, he would bug Tom. But deep down, Tom knew the kid was just looking for some attention because he never got it at home. It was actually difficult to call it his home. His dad married this woman and then dumped Bob on her and left.

She wanted Bob about as much as she wanted food poison or cancer. So, they all resented Bob for being dumped on them and took it out on him. Bob was a good kid but he needed a real home and he found one at our house and Tom seemed like a good candidate for a friend. I don't remember what ever happened with Bob. On my mother's last birthday before she died, we had a picture taken of everyone who was there and Bob is in that picture. He was just like a part of the family and it was all thanks to Tom for bringing home strays.

When Tom would want to go meet up with his friends, he didn't want to drag Bob along with him. To Tom, it was like having a little brother tag along and that's almost what Bob was like. He was like that annoying little brother. I don't think he was that much younger than Tom but they were close in age. Tom just wanted some time away from Bob. It was a difficult situation because Tom knew Bob needed a friend and needed some attention but he also knew he needed some time away from Bob.

Tom was his buddy and he simply attached himself to Tom. If Bob was at home and Tom was going to meet with his friends, he would have to sneak past their house. The path down to the highway went right past their house so Tom would hurry by and hope Bob didn't see him. We all felt sorry for Bob but he could be annoying some times.

Tom also had a friend who lived a short distance up the road in the opposite direction of Bob. His name was Terry Falcone. Tom would go up there and hang out with him but that didn't last long. Terry's parents were divorced and his mom worked fulltime so she was not always at home when Terry and his younger brother were there. That wasn't really a problem for Tom since they never got into anything that would get Terry's mom upset when she got home. But it was Terry's attitude and strange ideas about how to treat girls/women.

Tom came home one day from Terry's and began to tell me some of the stuff Terry was telling him about what he would like to do to women. The kid was demented to say the least and Tom never went back there and had nothing to do with Terry after that. I'm not sure that was the right thing to do since this kid could have evolved into a real scary guy and definitely needed some help. But Tom just wanted to get away from him. I can't remember if he told anyone else about this or not. You never know who is living around you.

Tom had other friends who were not demented but simply young boys who got into your normal boy type mischief. One I always remember had a nick name of Pickle. I'm not sure of his last name but I always remembered that nick name. Another boy was the brother of one of my closer friends. Dan McAdams was the brother of Kenny, one of my friends. Dan and Tom used to hang with each other quite a bit. They lived down across the highway and about a block down. The difference between Tom and me when we lived in Blairsville was, he didn't get into trouble like I did. I'm not going to go into the different ways I found trouble but Tom never came close. He was basically a good kid or he never got caught. No, he was a good kid.

So, Tom finally got a guitar. He didn't know how to play and our parents couldn't afford to have someone teach him. So, Tom just picked at it, studied it and listened to others play. He couldn't read music but he got pretty good doing it by ear. Once he learned the chords and where to put his fingers, he began to learn. I might've been out playing ball or doing something else and Tom would be home picking at that guitar. Our mom was afraid he would give up or become frustrated with trying to learn how to play and put it down and never go back to it. But not Tom. He stuck with it for years and he became a very good guitar player and song writer.

Now, I would have been the one to say, "I give up. This is too hard to learn." But Tom was determined to learn how to play. Like I said earlier, we both had a love for music and that played a big part in Tom's desire to learn how to play the guitar. I would walk into the bedroom and Tom would be in there picking at that guitar. The guitar wasn't a really good one but it was a guitar and he was determined to play it. His determination to learn that guitar was like mine was to be a better baseball player. He never allowed anything to discourage him. He would learn to play a brief riff and call me in and make me listen while he played it. But it would be quite a while before he could string together a song but when he did, he got very good at it. We'll come back to Tom's guitar playing later.

When Tom was too old for Little League Baseball, he never played in an organized league again. Baseball wasn't his thing.

But Tom told me something not long before he died that I had not realized or actually knew about. When he was still in junior high, he began to have an interest in scholastic wrestling. He even shared that interest with a wrestling coach. The coach informed him there were freshman who couldn't get on the mat and there was no way Tom could even get a look as a junior high student. But he was able to work out for the coach and get on the mat during a practice. He had had no training or instruction on any moves or techniques but he impressed the coach. The coach told him he had a great deal of potential but he could never get him on the team as a junior high student. Tom had found the sport he would excel at.

Tragedy Strikes

When Tom was thirteen and I was fifteen, our parents were involved in an auto accident which resulted in the death of our father. He wasn't killed immediately in the accident but lived for nine days following it. The doctors said it was a miracle he survived the accident at all but he did and years later I would understand why God gave him the extra time in this life. Our parents were both Christians but dad was kind of backslidden at the time of the accident. He was in intensive care and we were only allowed to visit him for five minutes every hour.

So, we took turns going in to see him. On one of those nine days, two of our uncles, my mother's brothers, who were Christian pastors, came to visit him. His room was down the hall from the waiting room and we could hear them asking him if he would repent. They returned after their five minutes with him and told us, "He has repented." I know my dad was in no danger of losing his salvation since that is not possible when we are saved. But God had given him the opportunity in this life to repent of his sin while living in a backslidden state. I know that those who are not Christians or believers in Jesus might think this is all a bunch of nonsense but it is dead serious business for every human being.

Tom and I were as confused and lost in the ability to understand how or why this was all happening. We were living at that hospital in Latrobe PA. The most devastating thing concerning the accident was that our mother had been driving. She was also in this hospital but on a different floor. We would spend time between her room and the waiting room on the ICU floor. Every day, a nurse would give us a report on our dad's condition and we continued to hope for his recovery.

But we were warned not to get too optimistic since he was still in critical condition. Tom and I would go in to see him together. His memory was damaged and he couldn't remember from one hour to the next what we might have talked about. He was able to recognize certain items and people but could not remember other information. It was definitely difficult for Tom and me to see him like that and five minutes every hour was not really enough time. Tom and I would take turns talking to him. I remember talking to him about a Pirate game I might have seen or heard. He recognized player names but when I would ask him about it the next time I went in, he wouldn't remember.

Our sister Vonnie was our transportation back and forth to the hospital and we spent most nights there. She was driving back and forth from Indiana PA which was about another fifteen to twenty miles farther. Tom and I just wanted life to return to normal. But that wasn't going to happen. On the morning he died, we were at home. We had decided to go home and get some rest after a nurse had given us a positive update on his condition. But early the next morning, the phone rang and it was the hospital telling us we needed to get back to the hospital as soon as possible because our dad had taken a turn for the worse. Our sister Myra called Vonnie and gave her the message and she would come as soon as possible. While we were waiting on Vonnie to get to our house in Blairsville, the hospital called again and ask when we were coming. Myra explained what the holdup was and the hospital urged us to get there as soon as possible.

What they weren't telling us was our dad had died that morning. They wouldn't give that information over the phone for emotional reasons and the risk of a traveling accident. When we got to the hospital and the ICU floor, we saw that his bed was empty and that's when a nurse informed us that he had passed away that morning. We were all stunned. We had received such encouraging news the day before and now he was gone. We were all in a state of disbelief and went down to our mom's room. Sad news and good news combined. She was being discharged that morning. A doctor had already informed her of dad's death. She was upset but I remember her handling it very well. It was as if she knew it was going to happen and maybe she did. She wasn't extremely emotional and talked to us about his death and she had a sense of peace about it.

Virgil, dad's son to his first wife, had been living in Maryland with his grandmother. Mom and dad, but mostly dad, had decided he couldn't tolerate Virgil constantly running away from home and being returned by the state police. He had to appear in juvenile court a few times and finally, the decision was made to take him back to his grandmother, his first wife's mother, when he was about sixteen. He had lived with her until he was about twelve but he was too much for her to handle so she told dad and he brought him into our family but Virgil acted like he didn't want to be a part of the family and his juvenile antics forced dad to take him back to his grandmother.

I said all of that to talk about Virgil's reappearance in our lives about two months before dad died. He had just returned from a tour in Vietnam with the Army. He showed up at our front door in uniform and his bags. Tom and I were kind of happy to see him but we did not know all about Virgil's baggage. He was a troubled person and dad didn't want him around. Mom and dad had been working grave yard shift. Myra went in to wake them and tell them Virgil was at the front door and wanted to know if he could come in. Dad told Myra, "Tell him to go away. I don't want to see him." But mom was more concerned about him and allowed him in. So, he stayed with us for a week or two until he had to report back in to an Army post which I can't remember.

He told us he had to go back and be processed out of the Army. I don't think he and dad were actually on good speaking terms during those two weeks. Tom and I listened to his war stories of how he was shot in the leg while in Vietnam but dad didn't want him talking to us about that. I was out one Saturday might messing around with some guys and one of the older guys sucker punched me and split my lip. It was a cheap shot but I simply took my licks and decided to go home. It was a short walk up the road to the house and when I went in, Virgil and dad were in the kitchen. Virgil looked at me and saw my lip and wanted to know what happened. I told him and he was ready to storm out of the house and go teach this guy a lesson for punching his little brother. But dad stopped him and said, "You're not going anywhere. Stay out of this." It wasn't said in a very nice tone and I sure didn't want this guy, who I hadn't seen in years retaliating for me.

So, for the two weeks Virgil was with us, he and dad didn't exactly become the long-lost son reunited to the loving father.

Tom and I kept our distance from them and when Virgil left, things went back to normal. Well, normal as we knew it.

Virgil was discharged from the Army and returned right after dad had died and was there for the funeral. He attended the funeral in his Army uniform and I remember him standing in front of me at the grave site and crying. He could be heard crying and I always wondered if he was sincere or simply putting on a show which he was always good at doing. I felt numb and wondered if I should be crying. I wasn't crying, didn't feel like crying and wondered if that was wrong. Tom told me he felt the same way. I think we were just numb to what was happening. That's all I remember about that day.

Virgil decided he was going to stick around and live with us. Our mom was strong, a strong woman. She had experienced a great deal of heartbreak and misery in her life but she was very strong for Tom and me.

Following dad's death and funeral, Tom and I would sleep on the floor in the living room. Mom would get up in the middle of the night and go into the kitchen and Tom and I would follow her. She would be sitting at the table and Tom and I had a ton of questions concerning death and where dad was or went after death. Mom would sit at the table and Tom and I would sit on the floor and she would answer our questions. We knew dad was dead but we were afraid we were going to see his ghost or something like that. Mom reassured us that would never happen. Mom knew what the Bible said about death and life after death.

So, our next question was, "So, where is he? Is he in heaven?" She then spent some time telling us about what the Bible says concerning a person's final destination. She told us our dad was saved, he was a Christian and a believer in Jesus. She told us how he would take his Bible to work on graveyard shift and read it at night since there was really nothing to do but sit and watch and be ready if a patient got up. We learned so much from her during those middle of the night talks. It was much better than anything I had learned in Sunday School.

She was such a big help for Tom and me as we were coping with this strange situation. We had so many questions and she had answers but if she didn't, she would tell us. She never gave us any feel-good answers which are empty and useless in those types of situations.

So, it was Tom, me, Myra, mom and Virgil. At first, Tom and I didn't mind Virgil being around but he began to act like he was going to replace dad in the home. He also began to get too chummy with mom as if she was his girlfriend instead of his stepmom. Tom and I really didn't like that. He began to order me and Tom around like he was our parent. He gave us more orders and scoldings than dad had in the previous year. Finally, mom told him to be quiet and let us alone. She told him he had no right to be ordering us around.

Virgil had found a job at the Indiana Hospital as a painter. He would catch a ride every morning with someone else who worked there. He would come home and clean up and then sit down next to mom on the sofa. Tom and I took note of this immediately. We talked to mom about this and she said she was going to tell him to sit somewhere else or get out. He insisted he meant nothing by it but we weren't buying that. Finally, mom told him he had to leave and he couldn't live there anymore. My memory of this is clear concerning mom telling him to leave but it also seems he was warned by someone else. For some reason, I seem to remember our older brother Link warning him to let mom alone and to stay away from her. But I'm not for sure about that even though I seem to remember someone telling him that.

So, Virgil was gone. He had met and eventually married a woman almost twice his age who also worked at the hospital. We thought he had a mother complex since he never knew his mom, was trying to cozy up to our mom and then married a woman nearly twice his age. Tom and I wouldn't see Virgil for almost another ten years.

Dad had died on June 11 1966 and that summer was strange. Everything was so different without dad around. It wasn't like he was very talkative or ever did much with us. But he was there and just that was comforting. And, knowing we could go to him whenever we needed something was enough. But he wasn't there anymore so we all struggled to make life the best we could. Myra was living with us and was working. Mom had gone back to work and when she was working second shift, Myra would make dinner for me and Tom.

Myra would catch a ride on the other side of route 22 at the onramp to the highway. One afternoon, her ride dropped her off there and she was hit by another car and ruptured her spleen.

It was like one thing after another but Tom and I were young teens and we were oblivious to some of this. We understood she was injured but didn't understand how bad. We were still numb to the death of our father and now this? I remember that she recovered and went back to work and continued to make dinner for us when she came home. Tom would sit alone in the bedroom picking at his guitar and I wondered if he was alright. He was thirteen years old and had just lost his dad. Tom was more compassionate and sensitive than I was back then.

When we were still living on Walnut Street in Blairsville, dad had quit his job working for the state and went halves with his brother on a fishing boat. That meant he went to the eastern shore of Virginia on the Chesapeake Bay where his brother lived. They were going into the commercial fishing business. Needless to say, it didn't work out to good. We went down to visit for a few days and dad took us out on the boat. He was a Navy Vet from WW II so being on the water was nothing to him. He had also grown up in that area.

When dad made the decision to cash in and come home, we didn't know anything about it. Tom and I were out in front of the house on the sidewalk and I looked up the street and saw dad coming, carry his bag. I told Tom, "Hey look, it's dad." At first Tom thought I was messing with him and then he saw dad and ran up to meet him. I went into the house and told mom that dad was coming down the street and she thought I was messing with her. I finally convinced her he was coming and Tom had run up to meet him and she made a beeline out the front door. When she got out the sidewalk and looked, there was dad with Tom coming close to the house.

It was memories like that which we had to hold onto. After dad's death, Tom was the one who was the better behaved son. I was the bad one. I caused our mom more trouble than she deserved. I won't go into detail but it seemed like she was always having to take care of a situation I had caused or was in some trouble with. Tom was a good kid; he didn't get into the trouble I did. Our mom wasn't having to always clean up any mess which he made because he didn't make any.

A few months after dad died, mom received a phone call one evening telling her that her mom had died. Tom and I were in our bedroom playing matchbook football. After we heard the phone ring, we heard mom let out a scream and we knew it was bad news.

We attended that funeral and it seemed like this was becoming a normal thing in our lives. Our mom took the death of her mother pretty good, considering what she had been through recently. Mom would take Tom and me on a run to Indiana for something and then she would always drive out to see her mom and dad. She did that when the opportunity presented itself. She would always tell Tom and me, “Now, don’t touch anything and sit and be quiet.” So, Tom and I would sit and only speak when we were spoken to. Her mom and dad were always kind and nice, never mean or grouchy. Grandpap was a good man and always talked to us and treated us good. But mom didn’t want us to act out or be unruly. We knew better than to do that because there would be consequences when we left.

Before dad died, we would take the trip down to the eastern shore of Maryland and Virginia where his family lived and where he grew up. We would stay at his father’s farm. His dad always grew cantaloupes and watermelon as well as a bunch of other stuff. But he would always take Tom and me and Myra out to his shed where there was a bench next to it and cut up a cantaloupe for us to eat. He was a good man and so nice to us. When Tom and I were about four and five years old, we were visiting one summer. Tom and I were running around dad’s car playing and I ran into a taillight and broke the lenses. Tom and I went inside to tell dad. He was talking to his dad and when we told him, he was trying hard not to show his anger. Grandpap told him, “It’s just a taillight Bill. There’s no need to get upset over that. I’m sure the boys didn’t mean to break it.” Then, you could see a calm come over dad and he agreed with his dad.

Before the Christmas of 1966, mom had asked me and Tom what we wanted. Tom and I both had talked about getting a bench warmer coat. They were a replica of what the football players wore on the sidelines during a game. Hence, the name bench warmer. We told our mom and she didn’t say yes or no. This would be our first Christmas without dad. Even though Tom and I were still early and mid-teens, we knew this Christmas would be different. It would be about six months since dad had died.

On Christmas morning, Tom and I opened our presents. I had been the one who had lobbied mom for the bench warmer coats and Tom was like, “Whatever.” He didn’t seem to be overly concerned about it and was just happy to have any coat.

So, when he opened his first and I saw it was a bench warmer, I was pretty excited and said, “Alright. You got us bench warmers!” I opened mine and it was a ski coat, the nylon puffy coat. I was stunned and asked mom, “Why does he get a bench warmer I get this? I’m the one who begged you for a bench warmer.” Mom told me, “I’m sorry. I couldn’t find one in your size.” She could tell I was disappointed but I thanked her for the coat and told her I understood. The worse thing I could do would have been to act like I didn’t appreciate the gift. I wore the coat and never said anymore about it. And, Tom wore his bench warmer and fit right in with all the other kids.

In the early months of 1967, Tom and I went to Indiana shopping with our mom. She took us to what would become my favorite clothing store, Waxlers. Waxlers was a boy’s and men’s clothing store and she bought Tom and me some new clothes. We didn’t ask for anything, she just wanted to buy us new clothes. While we were there, I noticed they had Navy Pea coats and it was becoming more popular than the bench warmer. Mom bought me the pea coat. We were both spoiled and it seemed that mom wanted to spoil us even more after dad died. Later that summer, she and Myra were downtown walking and she came up to me and handed me two five-dollar bills. She told me, “You give one of those to your brother when you see him. I’ve never been able to do that for you boys and now I can so make sure you give one to Tommy.” Now, keep in mind that five dollars in 1967 was like twenty dollars or more today.

I gave Tom his five dollars when I saw him later and he was as stunned as I was when mom handed them to me. Things seemed to be settling into a new type of normal and Tom and I were adjusting to it. Myra and her husband Russ had married in early 1967 and would eventually be relocating to just outside of Rochester NY where our oldest brother, Link, lived. He and Russ worked for the railroad there. But before Myra and Russ left, she would be the bearer of more bad news. The new normal was about to take a turn for the worst.

Tragedy Strikes Again

One morning in the Fall of 1967, Myra and I were in the kitchen in our home. She told me she had to tell me something about mom. She had a dead serious look on her face and I could tell it wasn't good. She went on to tell me mom had been to the doctor and was diagnosed with colon cancer. My first instinct was to deny it. I don't remember my exact words but it was something like I didn't believe it. Then, it was, 'she will be alright; she will beat this.' But then Myra gave me the really bad news: our mom only had about six months to live. That was the knock out punch and once again, I was simply stunned and numb all over again. I stood there quiet and didn't say anything. I was angry and frustrated and just didn't want to believe it or accept it.

I asked Myra if the doctor could be wrong but she said he wasn't and that even mom knew there was something seriously wrong with her. Then, she told me that mom wanted her to tell me but not Tom. Mom didn't think Tom could have handled that news at his age. Years later, he told me he had wished Myra or someone had told him. Eventually, we had to tell him. How do you tell a fourteen-year-old his mom is dying just over a year after his dad had died? I think it was me that finally told Tom because he began asking questions. He knew something was going on and it wasn't good. I couldn't keep it from him any longer.

I think Tom and I were both in denial about this. Our mom continued to work and had met another man who was a really good man. They enjoyed being around each other and he loved being around me and Tom. He enjoyed teasing us and trying to get under our skin with his little pranks and verbal jabs but we knew he was just messing with us.

His name was Paul and he would come by the house to see our mom and we had got along great. In the summer of 1967, before we got the bad news about mom, I had met a girl in Indiana and dated her for only a couple of weeks. I guess her parents didn't appreciate me and told her to send me packing. So, I went up to see her one night and she immediately told me it was over and done.

I used to hitch hike back and forth to Indiana and mom always told me if I couldn't hitch a ride to never call her to come and get me. (Back then, hitch hiking was relatively safe) I caught a ride to Homer City and was at the intersection of route 119 and 56 and I could usually catch a ride there but this night there was nothing. I was a heartbroken sixteen-year-old and by nine o'clock, I gave up and called mom. She said that under the circumstances, her and Paul would drive up and get me. There was no way my mother would ever have said no under any circumstances.

When she and Paul picked me up, Paul started right in on me. "So, your girlfriend dumped you? She didn't want you around anymore, huh?" I knew he was just trying to lighten the moment and make me feel better. Mom told him, "Stop it. He's hurting and that girl doesn't know what she has done." I told mom that her parents made her do it and then Paul jumped on that but before he could get started, mom put him in check.

Paul used to do that to both me and Tom. But Tom just ignored him where as I loved to banter with him. We all knew it was all in fun. Paul told mom that he wanted to take Tom and me shooting but she didn't like that idea. Tom and I were ready for that and eventually, Paul won her over. So, on a Sunday afternoon, Paul took us all out to an old out of use railroad bridge and had a 243-hunting rifle. He gave me and Tom some safety instructions and then allowed us to shoot. He pointed out some targets for us to shoot at and we began taking turns shooting. Paul enjoyed that time and so did Tom and I. Paul was a really good man to have around. I remember him being very serious one night when he told Tom and me, "I want you boys to know something. I would never attempt to take the place of your dad. I could never do that and I won't try. But I'm here if you ever need anything."

Tom and I never forgot that. Paul would never be able to replace dad but I don't think there could have ever been a better man in mom's life than him. He was the best.

So, it was so easy to think this could all be a mistake. Mom didn't look sick and she was still working and living like there was no problem at all. It was hard for Tom and I to accept the fact that she actually was running out of time. Paul kept coming around and he continued to take his jabs and we would go back and forth at each other. Life just seemed to continue on. Tom and I had our own little worlds we were living in. He had his friends and I had my girlfriends and Paul kept teasing me about them.

In December 1967, mom had to go into the hospital. Things were looking worse now. She was home for her birthday on the 21st and went in a couple of days later, right before Christmas. She spent Christmas in the hospital. Tom and I ate Christmas dinner at my girlfriend, Gloria's home. Her dad Nicky was all about hospitality and was happy to have us. Before mom's hospital stay, she was working an afternoon shift and told me if I was going to see Gloria that evening to take Tom with me because she didn't want him staying home by himself. Myra and Russ had moved to New York in October so she wasn't with us at home any more.

So, Tom and I walked over to Gloria's and when we went in, Nicky was glad to meet Tom and ask him if he was hungry. Tom, being shy, said no but Nicky wasn't taking no for an answer. It was a Wednesday evening and Wednesday in the Italian community was pasta night or spaghetti night. Nicky looked at Tom and said, "I know you are hungry because when I said we had springs (pasta) left over from dinner, your eyes got big and bright so I know you're hungry. Go downstairs and tell Gloria to fix you a plate of pasta." I had to keep from laughing when Nicky told him that. It was like a psychiatrist diagnosing a patient. So, Tom gave in and I took him downstairs to the kitchen and Gloria made him a plate and he ate all of it. I knew he was hungry because he had not eaten anything. We both ate pasta and sauce that night.

On another night when mom was in the hospital, she was concerned about us being at home by ourselves all night. Nicky volunteered his home for the night. Neither Tom nor I liked that idea but we couldn't wiggle out of it. We slept in a room with Gloria's younger brothers and left first thing in the morning.

Once again, Vonnie was our ride to the hospital in Latrobe. She would stop at the house in Blairsville and take us with her to visit mom.

Myra stayed with us for a while and Russ went back to New York to work. About the same time mom went into the hospital, Gloria's grandfather went in. One night, Nicky was visiting his father-in-law and decided to stop by mom's room for a visit. Gloria and I were in mom's room when Nicky came in to see how she was doing. Now, Nicky spoke in a very flat and boring monotone. It was alright for just a few sentences but if he decided to drone on and on, it was sleepy time. Mom appreciated him coming by to see her but told me, "Don't ever let him come in to talk to me again. It was all I could do to keep my eyes open." I started laughing and she told me she did think it was really nice of him to visit her but he did almost put her to sleep.

Gloria told me that her and mom had planned for us all, her family and ours, to eat Christmas dinner at her home but the hospital visit had ruined those plans. So, it was just Tom and me for dinner that Christmas with Gloria's family. It was nothing new for me since I ate pasta with them every Sunday but Tom was a little shy about the whole thing and Nicky kept making him feel welcome.

Mom was able to come home after Christmas and Myra was able to go back to New York with Russ. Things began to settle back in and Tom and I thought everything would be alright. But it wasn't long before mom began to get sicker and sicker as the cancer was taking a toll on her body.

Over the next six months, mom was in and out of the hospital and had at least one surgery. I remember standing outside her room when they wheeled her out to go to the operating room. As she went by, she grabbed my hand and told me she was afraid. I didn't know what to say. I was seventeen years old and she was my mom. I'm sure I mumbled something like, "It'll be alright mom." And then she was gone down the corridor to the OR. She survived that surgery but the doctor told us later they couldn't get all of the cancer and it was spreading too fast. We knew the end was coming soon.

Mom had told Paul not to come around anymore because she didn't want to put him through that. But he insisted he would be alright and just wanted to stay with her right up to the end. Mom told him no. So, Paul stayed away and didn't even attend the funeral. But years later, Tom was in a bar in Blairsville and Paul walked in. Tom got his attention and they sat and talked for a couple of hours. Tom said he was the same old Paul and it hurt him when mom died.

Sometime around March of 1968, mom was spending more time in the hospital and Vonnie and her husband Fred stayed with Tom and me for a week. But after one week, they had to go back to their home in Indiana. Myra stayed with us for a couple of weeks but she had to go home too. Finally, mom had to make a decision about Tom and me. We would have to go to New York and stay with Myra and Link. Tom stayed with Myra and I stayed with Link. Tom and I both fought this decision. We didn't want to be yanked out of school and moved to a new one this late in the school year. I was a senior and was getting ready to graduate and would have to spend the final two months of my senior year in a school where I would just attend the classes. I had more than enough credits to graduate in Blairsville so the school would allow me to return and graduate with my senior class.

I spent two months just showing up for class and being told not to worry about doing any class work since it was so late in the school year. The teachers were all understanding and just basically ignored my presence. Tom was enrolled in an elementary school in Fairfield NY where Myra and Russ lived. I attended East Rochester High School in East Rochester NY. It was a dismal final two months. Link would drive us back to Blairsville on some weekends to visit with mom. She was at home and we couldn't figure out why we couldn't just stay with her. She insisted she couldn't take care of us and we needed to stay in New York.

On Sunday afternoons we would be back on the road to East Rochester. Link tried to keep Tom and me together and occupied in something in the evenings. He would take us out to a park and hit flyballs to us or do something else to keep us entertained. I remember him taking us to a drive-in theater to see the first Planet of the Apes movie. We enjoyed that. I had a date to the prom back in Blairsville but couldn't make any arrangements from NY. I wrote letters to friends but never got an answer. Finally, Link told me he would be our chauffer. The girl I was taking was a girl I had dated after Gloria dumped me. I asked her to go with me before I was shipped off to NY and I couldn't tell her it was off. (I should have)

Everything went wrong; my tux was wrong; the pants were ripped in the rear seam and I think we both had a lousy time. Mom wanted to see us before we went to the school where the prom was being held.

So, Link drove me to Indiana to pick her up and then back to the house so mom could see us. Mom was really sick by this time. She had lost so much weight and looked like a skeleton with skin pulled over it. I knew that this girl was very uncomfortable with this whole scene but she was very understanding.

When Link drove back to Blairsville, Tom and I both were with him. It had to be hard on him making that drive back and forth and spending his weekends away from home. It wasn't every weekend but there were a lot of them. His wife, Louise, and their two boys, Ken and Jim, were also with us. The time always flew by and before we knew it, it was Sunday afternoon and we were back on the road to NY. Finally, it was time for my graduation. Link got me back to Blairsville and to my graduation. After the graduation ceremony, I stayed in Blairsville with mom. I remember Myra staying with us too.

Tom went back to NY and that was the beginning of a time when we didn't see much of each other. I was in Blairsville and Tom was in Fairport NY. My mom was dying and I was being a jerk. She would ask me to stay with her in the evenings and I'd run off to be with my friends. Finally, she went back in the hospital and didn't ever come home again. I would hitch hike to the hospital in Latrobe every day to see her. We talked about a lot of stuff and I then knew how important she had been in my life. I drew closer to my mother during those many visits. I knew her time was coming soon but her mind was still sharp and she had no problems carrying on conversations with me. We talked a lot and I tried hard to put her upcoming death out of my mind and just enjoyed the time we had together. I was back and forth every day and I didn't mind. Even on those days when I might have walked as far as I rode, I simply enjoyed being with her.

Tom didn't have those opportunities. He was in NY and only got to see mom on weekends. Finally, mom got really bad and I stopped going to the hospital. I didn't want to remember her that way. In the previous weeks, I had probably spent more time with my mom than I had in years. The last week she was alive, I stayed away from the hospital. On the night she died, everyone was there except me. I didn't want to see that. Tom was there and years later he told me he wished he had not been there and seen her like that.

I was at the house in Blairsville where I had been staying by myself.

It was about eight or nine o'clock when the phone rang and it was my Uncle Jack. He told me that mom had passed away. I had been expecting it so it wasn't really a surprise. He asked, "Are you alright? Are you going to be okay? Your brother and sisters are coming to the house and they should be there in a little while." Uncle Jack had taken care of everything for mom when dad died and had set up everything for when she died. So, everything had been taken care of by mom and him so it was just a matter of making the phone calls. Myra and Vonnie arrived at the house with Tom. The electricity had been shut off since mom had no money coming in before her death. We didn't care. I had been staying there in the dark for about a week. Uncle Jack's wife had given me twenty dollars for graduation and I had been using it for pizza and whatever else I needed. But after the funeral, that house would no longer be home. It hadn't been Tom's home for three months. Mom died on July 5th 1968. One day following the 4th of July.

Once again, Tom and I were attending a funeral for one of our parents. It was again numbness and frustration and hurt. Tom was hurting but not saying anything. He had kept dad's death bottled up inside for the previous two years and now he was facing the death of his mother and the loss of a home. I wanted to keep the house and continue to live there but that wasn't going to happen. Mom had a will saying the house would be sold with everything inside of it and the money put into a trust for Tom and me along with the life insurance money.

As the coffin was being carried out of the funeral home, Tom and I went out following it with the rest of our family. As I stepped onto the sidewalk, I looked to my right and there was Gloria. Her and mom had got along so well and really liked each other. She stood at a distance and watched as the coffin was placed in the hearse. Her presence registered but that was all. When the funeral was over, we all went to Indiana and to Uncle Jack's home. Uncle Jack had always been very close to our mom. Her death had a strong effect on him.

As the adults were discussing what to do with Tom and me, Link turned to me and said, "You have a choice. You can come to East Rochester with me and I'll get you a job at the railroad. Or, you can stay here with Vonnie and enlist in the military when you're eighteen." I was seventeen and didn't want to go back to NY. I wanted to stay in Indiana.

I wasn't in a frame of mind to make that kind of decision at that time. I couldn't even imagine going to work at the railroad. So, I made an emotional decision and told them I would stay and enlist in the military. All I was really doing was buying time. My friends were all in the Indiana area and that's why I wanted to stay.

When I gave Link my answer, someone asked where Tom was. I had seen him sitting on the curb outside the house and told them. We went outside and Link asked him what he was doing. Tom was crying and asked, "Where am I going to live now? I don't have a home anymore." Link stooped down and picked him up and told him, "Oh yes you do have a home. You're coming to live with me. My home is now your home and you are part of our family." Tom asked, "What about Bill?" Link then told him about my arrangements. I think Tom had just about everyone in tears. I knew exactly how he felt. We had lost the home we knew. Dad was gone and now two years later, mom was gone. It was just too much to digest emotionally.

That began a period of time when Tom and I didn't get to see much of each other. I had a friend, Terry, who I had enlisted in the Marines with and he and I took a road trip to east Rochester to visit. We were only there for a couple of days but it was time I got to spend with Tom and others in our family. Fred and Vonnie decided to also take a trip to East Rochester that summer and I went with them. We were there for about three or four days and when we headed back to Indiana, Fred's car broke down and Link came to tow us back to East Rochester. So, we were there for another couple of days until Fred was able to repair the car with Link's guidance.

Terry and I had enlisted in the Marines in October 1968. We were on a ninety-day delayed enlistment so our active duty didn't begin until January 2 1969. What a way to start a year. In May, I was home on leave for about twenty days before going to Vietnam. Tom and I were walking up to the middle of town and I had just finished infantry training. We forced marched everywhere at infantry school. That is a very fast paced walk and as we walked along, Tom asked me what the hurry was and it was then that I realized I had been walking like I was still at infantry school.

After stops at Camp Pendleton in California and then Okinawa, I was off to Vietnam for a year. I was not much of a letter writer so I didn't communicate with my family except Vonnie.

After a year in Vietnam, I returned home and left the Marines and wanted to start the next phase of my life. In the meantime, Tom had been attending East Rochester High School and had joined the wrestling team. He had finally found that sport at which he would excel.

The railroad shops in East Rochester had closed and Link and Russ took job transfers to Hollidaysburg PA. That's where they were when I came back from Vietnam and left the Marines. Tom had been under the teaching of good wrestling coaches at East Rochester and had learned a lot from them. He would take those skills to Hollidaysburg High School and get even better.

Tom and Bill in Iselin

Tom and Bill Blairsville 1962

Tom and Bill Little League 1963

Dad and mom Blairsville 1964

Tom and Bill Blairsville 1963

Tom and Bill with their dad 1963

Tom and Bill with their mom circa 1959

Tom and Ken March 1969

Tom with his guitar at Debbie Johnson's home circa 1971

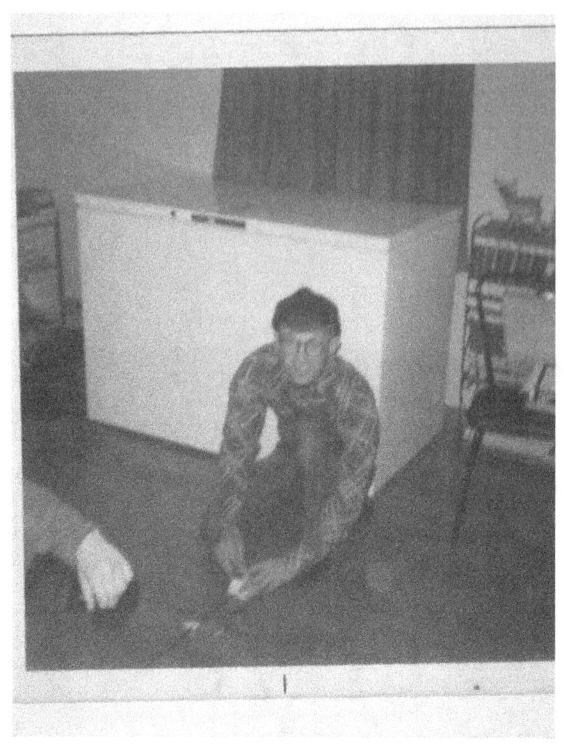

Tom home on leave from the Marines 1973

Life Moves On

When I returned from Vietnam, I was released from Marine Recruit Depot in San Diego CA. I was in Okinawa for six days and then on to San Diego for five more days while I was processed out of the Marines. Finally, the day came when I could fly home for the first time in a year. I flew into Pittsburgh and my whole family was there to greet me and drive me back to Indiana. On the ride from Pittsburgh, Tom and I talked the whole way home. We had not seen each other for over a year and we talked about a wide variety of topics. We had been so involved in our conversation we didn't realize we were already in Indiana. It was about a fifty-mile drive from the airport.

Tom spent the night at Vonnie's where I was living and we talked some more. It was quite the reunion. He told me about his wrestling and I answered his questions about the Marines and Vietnam. We had a couple of days together and then Link had to get back to Hollidaysburg and his job. But I considered that he was much closer now and visits could be more frequent. I had missed my little brother but in the next few years which followed, I was not going to be the example he needed to follow. I had repercussions from my tour in combat which I didn't even realize.

That Fall, Indiana High played Hollidaysburg High in football at Indiana. Tom said he would ride the bus to Indiana provided by the school and I would meet him outside the gate. So, we watched the game together and then he got on the bus and went back to Hollidaysburg. We got to see each other when Link would come to Indiana to visit Louise's family who lived there.

I had saved some money when I was in Vietnam and I used it to buy my dream car, a 1967 Chevelle. The only problem was, I didn't have a driver's license yet. I couldn't get it before mom died because her insurance was high following the accident.

So, I was just hoping I could get someone to let me do some driving when I got a driver's permit. I had a lot of issues. I was drinking too much alcohol and one night, Terry and I were out and we drank some beer and he wanted to drive my car. So, we went for a drive and when he turned around, I told him I wanted to drive back to town but he insisted he had to drive. We got into a scuffle and I gave in. When he parked the car, he got into his car and left. I didn't see him again for over thirty years. When he gave me my keys, I should have just gone inside and went to bed. But instead, I got in my car and drove away. I was intoxicated but not to the point I couldn't function. But I was impaired. I didn't even know where I was going. I drove down route 119 to route 22 and drove past Blairsville for about five miles and turned onto a secondary road. I was really tired and the booze didn't help. I dozed off and when I woke, I saw I was heading into a sharp curve. I overcorrected and ended up driving off of the road and into some trees. The car bounced back and forth off of the trees and the only part of the car which wasn't damaged was the truck lid. Link was in Indiana that weekend and when I called Vonnie, she called Link at Louise's mom's house
He and Fred came to get me and had contacted a local scrap yard and the owner agreed to tow the car and give me $25 for it. I wasn't too happy about that but this was all my fault. I was laid off at the time so when Link went back to Hollidaysburg, I went with him. While I was there, Myra's neighbor, who was actually her landlord, had a daughter who agreed to take me for my driver's test. I think she was a junior in high school and had a 1965 Mustang. I took the test and passed. I spent a week with Link and his family and Tom. Fred and Vonnie came down the following Sunday and told me I was called back to work. I was working for Fred's dad, a general contractor. I would be relocating to Hollidaysburg about eight months later.

It was good to be able to spend that week at Link's house and also with Myra and Russ. Tom and I got to spend the evenings together. We were both into music. Tom continued to work on getting better on his guitar and I had a desire to work in radio. We would both eventually achieve those goals. Tom would sit and listen to a song on the radio and learn how to play it on his guitar. That's how he learned, by listening and by ear. I couldn't play any kind of instrument but I never had a desire to. I messed around with the drums but never put my heart into it.

It was 1970 and '71. Tom's favorite musical groups and bands were Credence Clearwater Revival, Bread, Classics IV, The Eagles, Grass Roots and others. He could pick up on guitar chords and rhythms just by listening to these songs on the radio.

After spending a week at Link's, I went back to Indiana and back to work. I was earning minimum wage at the time and began saving again to buy another car. I still had a small amount in the bank and for the next four or five months, I saved almost everything I earned. The following March, I was invited to a party at one of the apartments for the students at IUP. It didn't end up well. I drank too much and then decided I was going to go to Cleveland OH to visit a friend from Vietnam. I went home and packed some clothes in a bag and began looking for my checkbook. Vonnie got up and came down stairs and was trying to talk me out of going to Cleveland. I was laid off again but was not in a good state of mind to be making these types of plans. I guess I got loud and Fred came down and told me to leave. I couldn't blame him. He had not asked to put up with that type of nonsense and middle of the night disturbances by a drunk. Vonnie gave me my checkbook and I walked up to the bus station and called Link. The trip to Cleveland was now forgotten and all I wanted was to complain to someone. Louise answered the phone and talked to me for a while and told me to stay where I was and Link would drive the fifty miles to Indiana and get me. The bus station wasn't open for business but the lobby was open and I sat in a booth and fell asleep. The next thing I knew, Link was waking me up. Russ had come with him and we got into Link's car and headed back to Hollidaysburg. I fell asleep on the way back and it was still early when we got back to Link's house.
What I didn't know, was Tom was wrestling that day. It was the first round in the State Tournament. He would be wrestling at the high school. I think he wrestled one match in the afternoon and another that night. I was a mess and Link told me about Tom's matches that day and asked me if I wanted to go. In my hazy mind I was able to comprehend what he was asking and I told him I wanted to go. He never told me I should go take a shower or clean up or even change clothes. The night before was a drunken haze and I wasn't really sure what had happened and what I had done. Louise was working and Link and the boys and I watched Tom wrestle.

I was not a big fan of wrestling but I enjoyed watching Tom when he wrestled. I just couldn't stand the thought of some kid's sweaty body all over me. My sports always involved some kind of a ball.

When the day matches were over, Link got up to leave and said, "Let's go. We'll stop at McDonald's and get some burgers. It sounded good to me. As we walked across the gym to the exit, it was then that I realized my jeans were ripped out in the butt. All the way up the seam. So, I walked across the gym to the exit with my butt hanging out for all to see. Now, I did have undies on but still. I asked Link if he knew my pants were ripped and he said he did. Then I asked why he didn't say anything and he told me, "I just thought it was a new way you kids were wearing your pants now." I kind of thought he was just teaching me a lesson. Kind of like, "You want to go out and get drunk and carry on, then you need to know what you look like." He didn't say that but it was his point, maybe. Again, it was my fault and my responsibility to know how to act and my actions and lifestyle in recent months were not exactly up to most people's standards.

We went back in to the school that night and watched Tom wrestle again. He had won his match earlier in the day and he won his match that night. Now it was on to the next round the following weekend. I had taken a shower and put on clean clothes before we went back to the school and I felt a lot better. Now, the younger brother was setting an example for the older brother to follow. Following mom's death almost three years prior to this time, the best thing that could have happened to Tom was Link taking him in. He had a good family life, a good and clean family life, and he was involved in a sport he really liked and was really good at. As a result of that, Ken and Jim were enthused by watching Tom wrestle and also became interested. I was really happy for Tom. He had sat on that curb outside of Uncle Jack's house that day and didn't think he had a home anymore. He had come a long way since that day and was doing great.

As we sat in the bleachers that evening waiting for the matches to start, Louise said, "Oh, there's Ted and Jeanne." My attention was drawn to the couple on the other side of the gym who were walking in front of the bleachers looking for a seat. Little did I know that night that Tom would be my best man at my wedding as I married that girl. That night, I didn't even know her but I would very soon.

The following weekend, Tom was wrestling in the next round at the Jaffa Mosque in Altoona. We all went in to watch him and on Saturday night, he lost his match and his high school wrestling career was over. It was a close match but he came up just a little short. He was disappointed but didn't let it bother him too much. The further in those rounds you go the tougher the competition. Tom had a lot of friends who would come and watch him and cheer him on. Some of them were girls he went to school with. On Saturday afternoon, a lot of those girls discovered I was Tom's brother and wanted to talk to me. I was about three years removed from high school and thought it was a little weird to think seriously about a high school girl. So, I simply answered their questions and didn't give it much thought.
That evening, following the matches, a few girls gathered around Tom and me and were asking Tom who I was and Tom introduced me. That is when I met Jeanne, the girl I would marry. So, Tom introduced me to my future wife. The following weekend we all went to see some kind of celebrity basketball game and I got to know her better and the rest is history.
I had to go back to Indiana and go back to work. But now, I also had to buy a car so I could drive to the Hollidaysburg area to see Jeanne. I used to walk past this used car dealership when I walked up town. I began to notice a 1965 Ford Galaxy and I stopped in and asked what the price was. The owner told me the price and I did have that much saved but I was hesitant. I needed my own car and finally, I bought the Ford and the next weekend I was on my way to Hollidaysburg.

It was really a good thing that I could drive to Link's home and spend the weekend with them and also see Jeanne. I would drive down Friday evening and drive back early Monday morning. Tom was dating a girl who lived across the road from Link. Her name was Debbie Johnson. They were pretty close but they eventually broke it off and Tom didn't see her anymore. Link had bought an old 1961 Chevy to drive back and forth to work so Louise had a car to get to work and back. Link would allow Tom to drive that old Chevy if he had a date or needed to go somewhere. But Link also expected Tom to learn how to take care of a car. So, he would have him check the oils and make some other checks.
Link was on him one day about checking the oil so Tom went out to check the oil on the old Chevy.

It needed a quart added and Link was trying to figure out why it was taking so long just to add a quart of oil. So, he went out to see what Tom was doing and found him trying to add oil by pouring it down the dipstick tube. Another time, when Tom had purchased his own car, Link told him to check and see if the ball joints need lubed. Tom decided the ball joints needed lubed so when Link went out to check on how he was doing, he found Tom rubbing grease all over the outside of the ball joints. The proper way is to use a grease gun and pump the grease into the inside of the ball joint. And finally, I had bought some reverse shackles for the leaf springs on a car I owned. After I had installed them and disposed of the stock parts, I learned they were illegal. So, I decided to just remove the reversed shackles and cut them down. I asked Tom to help me cut them while I reinstalled the ones I had already cut.
He said he would. I was wondering what was taking him so long to get the last two cut when he came out and told me he couldn't get the last one cut and said he had to get ready for a date. He handed me the hacksaw and the shackle and I couldn't believe what I saw. The side of the blade where there was supposed to be teeth was as smooth as the top side. It was no wonder he couldn't get the last shackle cut since there were no teeth left on the saw blade. Tom was a very good wrestler and was quickly learning the guitar but he was not mechanically inclined.

I think it was in August of 1971 when Jeanne's dad set me up with a job in the Hollidaysburg area. E.J. Hallow was an older man who owned a lot of land in the Hollidaysburg area. He was selling it to a builder who was building houses on the land. He had the old guy come out to the house (at this time Jeanne and her family lived right up the road from Link). He introduced me to E.J and the next thing I knew he was driving me to Hollidaysburg to meet the builder. It was a Sunday afternoon and I was thinking that even if this guy was looking for help, it'll never be me after disturbing him on a quiet Sunday afternoon.
E.J. knocked on the builder's door and he came to answer it and recognized it was E.J. and questioned as to why he was there. E.J. had me introduce myself and Duff, the builder asked me what my qualifications were. I told him what I had been doing for Fred's dad and for how long. He asked me a few more questions and then asked me, "Are you related to Tom Petitt, the wrestler?"

I told Duff I was his brother and the conversation quickly turned to wrestling. Duff was a big high school wrestling fan and was a big fan of Tom's. Duff was strictly business until he asked me about Tom and then he acted like we were old friends. When we were finished, he promised me nothing and thanked me for stopping by. About two weeks later, on a Sunday afternoon, Jeanne and I returned from being out somewhere and I was told that Louise had called and needed me to call her. I called her and she told me, "You need to come down here. There is someone here who wants to talk with you."

She didn't tell me who it was and I jumped back in my car and drove the short distance down the road. I saw the strange car in the driveway and when I went in the house, it was Duff sitting at the kitchen table with Link talking about wrestling. When they stopped, Duff looked at me and asked, "Are you still looking for a job? If you are, I have one for you." I had never given it a second thought when I left Duff's house that Sunday afternoon. I just considered E.J. was some crazy old man who had intruded in this guy's life on a Sunday afternoon and Duff wasn't even hiring. I never gave it a second thought that Duff would offer me a job but he was a big wrestling fan and a big fan of Tom's. So, Tom not only introduced me to my future wife but he also got me a job in the area so I wouldn't have to make the fifty-mile drive one way from Indiana to Hollidaysburg.

Marines

In the summer of 1972, Jeanne and I had set our wedding date and Tom agreed to be my best man. There was no other choice; it was going to be Tom or no one. Tom was working at a gas station on Blair Street in Hollidaysburg. It was actually Route 22 running through town. The station was open twenty-four hours and the owner had Tom working graveyard. Even though the station was located on the main thoroughfare through town, he saw very little business. So, Tom basically just sat all night waiting for someone to stop. He would do other little things but nothing to really keep busy.

Jeanne and I had rented an apartment in town and one night I was staying there and decided to drop by and visit with Tom and break his boredom. He was just trying to find something to stay busy with. He just showed me around the place and told me what he was supposed to do in between customers. But the time in between customers was hours and nothing there could keep him that busy. I hung out with him for a while and then decided to go get some sleep. The owner of the station accused Tom of stealing money from him. Tom denied stealing anything from the guy and he was fired. Tom was angrier about being accused of stealing than losing the job. I knew Tom wasn't a thief and he didn't steal the man's money. We never did find out what was going on there but Tom was glad to get away from a guy like that.

On the day of our wedding, I asked Tom, as my best man, to drive us to the reception in my car. He drove us away from the church on a secondary road which led to Route 22. When he pulled out onto 22, there was a tandem axled dump truck barreling down on us. Jeanne and I were sure our wedding day was also going to be our death date. Tom hit the throttle and got out of the way just in time. We were scared but we laughed about that moment for years. But that fit perfectly with the way Tom lived and did things.

During this same time, Tom received a draft notice. At the time, the draft was being conducted by some kind of lottery and I never did understand how it worked. Your draft number would come up but it didn't necessarily mean you would be drafted. When I enlisted in the Marines, the draft was simple. You get a draft notice in the mail and you're drafted and had to report. But this all changed since the time I was enlisted.
So, Tom started to consider his options and knew he didn't want to be in the Army so he went to see the Air Force recruiter. There must be something about Air Force recruiters that makes them keep you dangling. Tom was trying to get this guy to get his enlistment paperwork started so he could get enlisted before he got a notice to report. But the guy kept making excuses as to why there was a delay. The same thing happened to me and Terry when we decided to enlist. The Vietnam war was raging and we thought we would take the easy route and go to the Air Force and play it safe. But that Air Force recruiter did the same thing. He strung us along and strung us along until one day we were in his office waiting for him and the Marine recruiter walked in and told us what the guy was doing. He was keeping us on hold until he needed to fill his quota for the month. He then talked us into enlisting in the Marines.

So, Tom was losing patience. I never attempted to influence Tom one way or the other and considered this to be his decision. But when he began to tell me about what was going on, I stopped him and told him, "Forget this guy and the Air Force. If you want to enlist, go to the branch you will always be proud of. Go to the Marines and you won't regret it." Tom went to see the Marine recruiter and enlisted in the Marines. He never said a word to the Air Force recruiter just like Terry and I never talked to that guy who was stringing us along.
I was at Link's on the day the Air Force recruiter called. He wanted to talk to Tom and Louise told him Tom was working. Then he told Louise who he was and she was quick to tell him Tom had enlisted in the Marines because he was tired of waiting on him. The guy didn't like that and Louise finally had to tell him it was final and never call there again. I guess he was pretty upset and was getting a little belligerent with her. When she hung up the phone, she told me what he was saying and I told her it was a good thing I didn't answer the phone.

Tom loved the Marine Corps and never regretted his decision. He just didn't like the job he had as a Marine. When he was initially assigned an MOS (military occupational specialty), he was going to be a cook. Well, that isn't what he wanted. He was told he could talk to a career counselor and get it changed. So, Tom talked to the counselor and he was told he could work for the provost marshal but Tom didn't know what that was. The counselor gave him a rosy picture of what an MP (military policemen) was and told him he would be working with troubled Marines. Tom thought it was some kind of cushy desk job but would soon find out he had been deceived.

He was on a two-year enlistment and when he agreed to accept the new MOS, the counselor slid a piece of paper across the table and told him to sign it. Tom thought it had to do with his new MOS but when he gave it back to the counselor, he was told he had just added another year to his enlistment. So now he was enlisted for three years instead of two but he considered it well worth it not to be a cook. He told the counselor he didn't enlist in the Marines to be a cook. But I'm also pretty sure he didn't enlist to be a cop either.

The two-year enlistment program was an enlistment they used to entice people to enlist during the Vietnam conflict. It was what sold me. My thought was two years of my life was better than four. I was surprised they still had it when Tom enlisted.

Before Tom had to report, he was working for a small-time contractor by the name of Tim Drass. In simple terms, he was a crook. He would give you a big sales pitch on how much money you were going to make working for him but the problem was he never paid you. I found this out the hard way. I had been sucked into his lies when I was out of work and looking for a job. He told me he would line up the work and I would work as a subcontractor and do the work. But he kept switching my role from a sub to an employee. Then I began a siding job for him and was halfway through and told him if he didn't pay me for what I had done, he could finish the job and I was leaving. He paid me a portion of the work but not what I was due.

One day on that job, a guy stopped by and asked me if it was a Tim Drass job. I told him it was and he told me to walk away because I would never get paid. He said he was speaking from experience. When I showed up the next day, all the material was gone.

I guess the guy was still owed money by Drass and he decided to take the material as payment. He never paid me all that he owed me and I had to walk away. But I would sit on the steps of his house everyday waiting for him to come home so I could bug him. But he stopped coming home until after I had left and I finally accepted he was never going to pay me and chalked it up to a life experience just as the guy who had stolen his material had done. One former sub broke into his office and went through his files and then reported him to the IRS. The IRS audited him and discovered he had not paid taxes and they red tagged everything he owned until his debt was paid. He had burned so many guys and their payback was costly. Material was stolen from job sites, the IRS thing and belts on his truck were cut. His reputation was well known as a crook and someone not to be trusted.

So, when Tom told me he was working for this guy, I told him to quit because he would never get paid. Tom said he had got paid and he was doing some grunt work for him like digging ditches and other menial stuff like that. Then he said, "I'm not going to be there much longer because I'm going to quit about a week before I go. He made out better than I did. Drass paid him what he owed him.

I think it was in September of 1972 when Tom left for Parris Island and he would soon experience a lot of what I had about three years before. Tom never regretted his decision to enlist in the Marines. For the rest of his life, he was proud to have served with the Marines. Even if he was an MP, which were widely disliked by other Marines, he still was proud of his service and being a Marine. From experience, I know there is something special about having been an active-duty Marine.
Tom did all the duties of a Marine MP. He did gate duty, patrol, dog catcher and even undercover work. When he was enlisted, the Marine Corps didn't have their own MP training so they were sent to the Army MP school at Ft Steward, GA. Tom said when he got off of the bus at Ft Steward, he had to walk all the way across post to get to his barracks. He said he was harassed all the way by Army guys yelling out the windows of the buildings at him. He just smiled and kept walking. He knew who he was and never allowed it to bother him. When he left MP school, he was assigned to Marine Air Station, Beaufort, SC.

So, Tom had not traveled far. He had gone to Parris Island and in the middle of boot camp was taken to Camp LeJeune NC for three weeks of infantry training and then returned to Parris Island to complete boot camp. Following boot camp and some leave time, he went to Ft Steward and then right back to Beaufort to the Air Station which is actually a stone's throw away from Parris Island. He didn't actually see the world.

Toward the end of his enlistment, he was involved in an undercover drug bust in the NCO club on base. He made a buy from a dealer in the men's room. The dealer was busted but Tom's identity was exposed and his MP unit did a terrible job of trying to protect him. So, as an MP, everywhere he went he had two other MPs with him as body guards or escorts. After a while he was placed on animal control and finished his time as a dog catcher. He didn't mind doing that job but was always just a little bit irritated by the way his unit botched his safety following the drug bust.

He told me about the crazy and scary situations he was involved in when dealing with some bad guys. Like trapping a Marine in a mobile home who had a side gig as a hired hit man. This guy was killing people for $50.00 a pop. Tom did his job and was well respected by his peers and his leadership. He loved the Marines but hated being an MP.

During his time in boot camp, Tom was selected to be one of two guys who would spend a day at motivation. I realize that I am regressing in this timeline of events but this is an unforgettable event. Motivation platoon was a special place at Parris Island where problem children were sent for a day, a week or longer depending on the offense. But early in training, the Drill Instructors would randomly select two recruits to go to motivation for a day so they could return that evening and tell the others what they experienced. As fate would have it, Tom was one of the two examples sent out to motivation. He told me they ran about five miles and then were told to stop and take a break. The break consisted of doing numerous side straddle hops. We did thousands of these things in normal training so I can only imagine how many they were doing on their break. He told me they had to get into the sewage ditch coming out of the mess hall and begin to walk through it. But before they were finished, he said they were swimming in it because it was so deep. That must be why when our two guys returned, their uniforms weren't green anymore but instead, they were gray.

Our Drill Instructor told the two recruits from our platoon to tell us what they experienced. He told them to put it as plain and simple as they could so we would get a very good understanding of what they had experience that day. We heard them loud and clear and from the way they looked and what we heard, most of us wanted no part of that. I say most because there is always one or two who have to learn the hard way and we had one.
We don't know why the Drill Instructor had picked the two recruits he did. And of all the luck, Tom was picked as one when he went to Parris Island. I know I wanted no part of that experience and Tom never wanted to experience it again. There were a lot of different types of disciplinary activities at Parris Island but motivation had to be the worst. Unless a recruit deserved correctional custody platoon but that's another story.

Tom breezed through boot camp and then came home on leave before going to MP school. Link, Russ and I went to Harrisburg to the airport to pick Tom up when he came home. Link drove and Tom landed in Harrisburg at about 11 PM and on the ride back, we swapped stories about Parris Island and what we had each experienced. We laughed the whole way home telling those stories. At the time it was happening it might not have been funny or you couldn't laugh but retelling those stories were really funny. Actually, Tom and I could laugh about the stuff we experienced there for years. It never failed that when we talked, the conversation always came around to our experiences in the Marines and the funniest stuff was always about Parris Island.

Tom and I would talk on the phone periodically while he was stationed at the Air Station but most of the time it was hard to catch him off duty. He came home on leave a few times but those were brief visits. Tom left the Marines in 1975. He really did love the Marines but he despised being an MP and decided to go back to civilian life. I was working for a company which had sold above ground swimming pools and storage sheds. The two owners decided they wanted to get into the vinyl siding business. They were hiring people with any kind of building construction experience so I applied and they hired me. They told us if we knew of others looking for work to tell them. So, I asked Tom if he wanted to work with me doing siding and aluminum soffit and facia.

He told me he would and these guys hired him. But Tom was slow, really slow. I tried to get him to move a little faster but he was inexperienced and I didn't want to push him too hard. We were doing a garage in Altoona and the owner stood and talked to us all day long about anything. We were distracted and I forgot to wrap the building with foil. We finished the garage and Tom mentioned we had not put the foil on. I told him, "You're right. That guy stood out here every day yapping and I totally missed the foil. Well, he didn't say anything about it and it is an old garage. Maybe he didn't even notice."

When Tom and I showed up the next day, the boss told us the guy had called and complained about no foil on the building. I explained what happened and the boss told us to go back and rip off the siding and redo it all and put the foil on. So, Tom and I did just that but that guy never came out of his house while we were there. It took about half the time when we redid it because we had no distraction. I should have known better but I allowed that guy to totally distract both of us.

We moved on to a house in Lakemont and it was siding and soffit and facia. I cut and bent all the aluminum and Tom installed it. This was after we had done the siding. But it was really slow because Tom had never done this kind of work before. We were told to go back to the shop at the end of the day for a meeting. I knew we were behind on this job and should have been finished. When we got back to the shop, we were given pink slips. Almost everyone who worked there was given a termination notice. The guy who was forced to hand them out had been hired a few days before me. He schmoozed his way into a foreman's job but he was a crook. He sold these guys his radial arm saw and then stole it back from them. He would come around to check on us at job sites in the boss's new Chevy with a beer between his legs.

Now, he was forced to hand out termination slips. Not reduction in force layoff slips and the last Tom and I saw of him, he was backed into a corner by about ten of the guys who had received a pink slip. These two guys were trying to pull a fast one on us. Instead of laying us off, they were firing us in order to keep their unemployment tax down. Of course, it didn't work and we all filed protests and won the right to file for unemployment compensation. They had gotten in over their heads financially with the vinyl siding work.

While Tom was at the unemployment office, he was offered the opportunity to attend a state funded class for welding. He accepted and was placed in a welding class at the Altoona Vo-Tech School. During the school year, these classes were held at night and during the summer months, they were held during the day. Later, I would attend one of these classes for Technical Drawing.

While Tom was attending this class and learning to weld, he met a girl. We'll call her Kathy. Tom really fell for this woman but she was a little stand offish. But Tom was persistent and finally was able to win her over to a degree. Tom was drinking too much alcohol for her liking and told him he had to stop or she wouldn't see him anymore. On an early Sunday morning, my phone rang and it was Kathy. She asked me if I would come up to Tyrone to her house and drive Tom home. I told her I would be there as soon as I could and headed for Tyrone. When I arrived, Tom was passed out and couldn't be wakened. Kathy was a very mechanically experienced woman and told me she had pulled his distributor wire so his car wouldn't start. Then, she told me she would take care of him when he woke up and get him sober and replace the distributor wire. She apologized for having me drive up there for nothing but I told her it was not a problem and to take care of Tom. Following that episode, Tom showing up at her house in the middle of the night drunk, she refused to ever see him again. He got over it but lost a good woman as a result. Kathy wanted more than anything to be with Tom but would not tolerate his drinking habit.

I felt bad for Tom and had even encouraged him to stop drinking if he really wanted this woman. There was more to it than that. At first, she wanted nothing to do with Tom or any other man in that class. If I remember correctly, she had a small son and was being very careful who she would bring into his life. She sincerely tried to make Tom work but had to turn him away as a result of his drinking. I couldn't say I was any better. I had my own problems with alcohol at that time. Tom and I had a few drunken nights together.

Tom finished his welding class and was ready to get a job welding. He applied at several locations and one day got a call from the state. It was a crew who made repairs to bridges and overpasses. They told him where to meet them the following morning.

It was close to where Tom was living so he met the crew at a small bridge which needed repaired. The foreman told him what needed to be welded and it was one of the most difficult welds to make. It was an overhead weld. Tom made the weld and it met the satisfaction of the foreman. Tom worked with that crew all that day and thought he had finally landed a good job. But at the end of the day, he was thanked for his time and told they weren't really hiring. What a gut punch. Tom expressed his opinion of that and left.
Tom was eventually hired by Altoona Pipe and Steel and worked there for many years. He enjoyed welding and steel fabrication.

The recession of the 1970s was bad. Jobs were really hard to come by but Tom had a job which kept him employed. I, on the other hand, experienced layoff after layoff until there came a time when there was no call back. Finally, I landed a job at a local state park. It was a special program for unemployed workers. These jobs were state funded and I was employed by the state. I interviewed and got the job and enjoyed the work. But I also knew it wasn't a job which would be a career maker. I had applied for a class similar to what Tom had attended. I received a call telling me I was accepted for the class and decided to attend. I would have to quit my job at the state park in order to attend and that's what I did. We were told a survey had been done and there was a demand for draftsmen within a 100-mile radius of Altoona. That proved to be false. When I finished the class, I went as far as Philadelphia to find work. There were openings but wouldn't hire anyone without experience. That was so frustrating; I couldn't even get an interview if I had no experience. I told these places I had drawings which they could look at but it was no deal.

I went back to Altoona and was at a loss as to what to do next. I had quit a steady job at the park for this and now it turned out to be a bust. I was going through the want ads one day looking for work and saw an ad for draftsmen. I called the 800 number and it turned out to be the Army. That got me thinking about a return to the Marines. I talked to Jeanne and explained that we would have a roof over our heads, food on the table and medical. And the job would be steady with no more layoffs. She agreed and I got the ball rolling.

In the meantime, Tom was working at Pipe and Steel and doing good. He had his own place and was treated like a son by his landlady. She would bake for him and bring him meals. She was actually spoiling Tom. Eventually, I went back into the military (the Army and that's a sad story for another time). As mentioned earlier in this book, Tom always had a thing for strays, human and dogs. He was conned by a woman he met. She fed him lie after lie and spent his money. She told him she was pregnant and that it was his baby but she wasn't pregnant at all but instead had a medical problem which looked similar to a pregnancy. She was older than Tom and Louise tried to tell him this woman wasn't pregnant but he wouldn't listen.

Louise worked at a department store in Hollidaysburg and the Greyhound bus would stop right in front of that store. Louise was working the checkout at the front of the store and saw this woman with her bag getting on that bus. She knew she was running off with Tom's money. Tom and I had a trust which was set up by our mom before she died. It was managed by a bank in Indiana PA and we received a disbursement every November from the interest accumulated for the year. It was paid out annually until we reached the age of thirty. Tom wasn't thirty yet and Louise knew that was the day the checks were to be in our mailboxes. She also knew, when she saw that woman getting on that bus, that she had Tom's check from the trust.

Louise was right. I received my check that day but Tom's was gone. This woman had grabbed it and ran away with it and Tom never saw her again. She had conned him the whole time. He learned a very hard lesson from that experience but was still not out of the woods with bad women or strays.

Dark Times and Overcoming

I was stationed at Fort Bliss in El Paso Texas. We liked the climate there because it wasn't freezing cold like PA. While I was there, I lost track of Tom and didn't know what he was up to. We traveled back to PA in May of 1978 and Tom introduced us to his new girlfriend, Patty. When he first mentioned her, I was hoping she was the right person for him. He had not had much luck with girls or women. Debbie Johnson had teased him with sex and then shut him down. The frustration was too much for him so he walked away from that relationship. Then it was Denise. She was a good person and she and Tom got along really good but something happened and I think it was her who walked away from Tom.

So, now it was Patty. When Jeanne and I met her, we knew something wasn't right. She was in her twenties but acted like a fifteen-year-old. I immediately realized she wasn't acting but she really did have the mind of a woman much younger than her age. She was mentally challenged. It is a mental defect which has affected many people. But Tom didn't see it and he was happy with her the way she was. I just considered it his business and didn't think it was my place to tell him he was wrong. As long as everything was alright and they could live with each other like that.

But that wasn't the case. When I left the Army and returned to the Hollidaysburg area for about ten months, her and Tom were living in Greenwood just outside of Altoona. Patty had had a baby girl and Tom was in his glory. But he soon discovered Patty couldn't take care of the baby. The baby would grow and have some difficult early years as a result of her mother's mental condition. The baby girl would also have these same mental issues but Tom was always there for her. They eventually separated (I don't think they were ever married) and Patty took the baby girl. Tom would eventually win custody of the his daughter when she was about twelve years old. But before that time, things were rough.

I had gone back to El Paso due to a lack of jobs and no work. I had to be able to support my family and life in PA wasn't giving me that opportunity. Tom told me years later that he just couldn't believe I had packed up and traveled over half way across the country with my family. I explained to him I had no choice. I had to be able to support my family and there were jobs in El Paso.

I didn't talk to Tom for about the next year and by that time I was working at the National Training Center at Ft Irwin CA. We had moved on from El Paso when I discovered this job and was hired. So, again we were on the move. It was a very good paying job and I was finally able to provide for my family without squeezing pennies. I was told we were going to be getting welders in our shops and the jobs would soon be opening. I talked with my maintenance chief and told him about Tom. He told me to tell him to get his resume to him and he would hire him.
I called Tom and told him but he said he couldn't do that. He was trying to win the custody of his daughter, Crystal, and couldn't leave the area. I explained it paid more than he had ever made but he just couldn't leave without his daughter. I understood and didn't push it anymore. It would have been nice to have had Tom in CA with me but it wasn't meant to be.

Jeanne and I were in bed one night and the phone rang. It was Tom; Jeanne handed me the phone and told me it was Tom but he sounded strange. I asked Tom what was going on and he began to rant about people chasing him. He said, "They're after me. They've been chasing me all night. They were in a bar I was in and now they are after me and I can't get away." At first, I just thought he might be drunk and imagining it all. I tried to calm him down but he continued his wild rant about people always chasing after him. I began to realize this was more than a drunken imagination. I didn't know what to say so I told him to lock his doors and go to bed. It was about midnight in CA so it was close to three in the morning in PA. This was after I had talked to him about the job and he had seemed fine then. But something was seriously wrong now and I was all the way on the other side of the country and couldn't help him.

I spoke with Louise and told her about his phone call and she explained that Tom had been staying away. That wasn't like Tom.

He was always at Link's place because that was his home. Louise told me they saw him walking along the road one day. He had turned and seen them coming and jumped over the guardrail and hid in the weeds. She told me they wanted to help him but he wouldn't make himself available. My sister Myra recently told me that Tom was experiencing a mental breakdown and they were finally able to get him into the hospital.

For the next several years I didn't have much contact with Tom. He finally did get custody of his daughter and he took care of her. He had rescued her from a life that was and would have continued to be terrible. Tom worked hard to support her and take care of her. She was involved in and won several gold medals in the Special Olympics as a runner. I remember jokingly telling Tom, "Well, she has the good genes for it." She was a very good athlete and Tom was really proud of her. I remember when she worked in a food processing plant that made pretzels. Her shift began at four in the morning and Tom was up to take her to work every morning. He was a terrific father to her. I've known many fathers who would have never done that for their kids.

Tom had recovered from whatever his breakdown had been caused by. He continued to work as a welder and provided for his daughter as she grew into a young woman. His dark time had come to an end and he had made a good life for him and his daughter. He continued to get better and better on his guitar. That was something which remained a constant with Tom regardless of his life situation. There were always two things which stood out in Tom's life; his skill as a wrestler and his talent as a guitar player. He left his wrestling skills behind when he left high school but continued to be a fan. But his talent and skill with the guitar continued to excel as he grew in years. Tom would go to retirement homes and play for the residents. At times, he would play and sing with a local gospel group in local churches. He enjoyed being the entertainer but not for himself but for those he could entertain.

Jeanne and I returned back to the Altoona area in May of 1999. Tom had met and married Julie. Julie had two sons to a previous marriage and Tom attempted to treat them as his own but that proved to be difficult in the beginning.

Taking on two teenaged boys can be a difficult situation. Tom never tried to act as their father and he never attempted to rule over them with an iron fist. He simply wanted them to abide by the rules of the home which he and Julie put forth. There were a few challenging times when the boys were outright rebellious and refused to listen to Tom but eventually they came around.

Not long after we returned, the youngest of the boys took his life. Tom called me on a Sunday morning and filled me in and Jeanne and I went to Tom's house to talk with them. Of course, there were all kinds of questions about the boy's final destination following his death and those are hard questions to answer when you don't personally know the person. I did my best to answer those questions and comfort them both. But those are difficult situations and for Tom, it was just like he had lost a son that was biologically his. That youngest son had come to love and respect Tom and realized that Tom only wanted what was best for him. Sadly, he had taken his life as a result of being rejected by a girl. I am so glad I could be there for them both. Many times, that's all that it takes. Just be there; no fancy words or cliches just be there for the grieving parents.

Tom had left Altoona Pipe and Steel and was working in a fabrication shop in Tipton. Tipton was about ten miles north of Altoona. Tom had just bought a pickup truck and on his way to work one morning, a deer ran out in front of him and he hit it. The truck was a loss and he hadn't had it but a few days or maybe a week. It was taken care of and he was able to replace it with another truck. Tom enjoyed his work in that fab shop and was good at what he did. But eventually, the shop would have to close its doors and Tom would be moving back to Pipe and Steel.

My oldest daughter Michelle and my son, Joe, also relocated to PA in 1999. Any time one of the grandkids had a birthday celebration, we always invited Tom and Julie to join us. While I was living in the Altoona area, I tried to see Tom as much as I could. We would get together and just talk. We talked about our years growing up and the people and friends we knew. We'd talk about work and we always discussed the Marines and our experiences with them. We could talk about the Marines for hours and it never got old.

We would laugh about the stunts the drill instructors pulled on us at Parris Island and that was as funny every time we talked as it was the first time. And, we talked about Jesus and His work in our lives. Those were great times together. We had been best friends all of our lives and even in those long stretches we had when we were geographically apart, we never grew apart in our relationship as brothers.

Three years after returning to the Altoona area, I took a staff position with an inner-city ministry in Lancaster PA. It was about three hours from Altoona and Tom and I didn't see each other as often. We would occasionally make the trip back to the Altoona area for a weekend but still didn't see each other that often. We would stay with Link and Louise or get a hotel room. There were times when we knew we were going back there for a weekend and I would try to give Tom a heads up but many times, he had previous plans. I can say this; Tom didn't allow any grass to grow under his feet in his off time. He kept busy on most weekends gathering with friends and watching local bands play. He enjoyed camping during the warmer months and spent many weekends at various camping grounds. So, many times when were visiting in the Altoona area, he and Julie were camping that weekend.

Jeanne and I stayed in the Lancaster/York area in southcentral PA until I retired. So, the only times I got to see Tom was when we went for a weekend visit. But there was one time when Tom and Julie traveled to our area of the state and spent a night in Lancaster. They were touring the Amish country which was very populated east of Lancaster. Tom called and told me they would be there Friday night to stay and wanted us to meet them for breakfast on Saturday morning at the hotel. Of course, we agreed and met them for breakfast. That was a good time and we enjoyed catching up with each other. I gave him some directions and the best places to see in that area and then we went our separate ways.

Tom and I attended the wedding of a niece of ours. At the reception, Tom and I sat at the same table and had a chance to talk for the first time in a while. Tom looked at me and said, "You know, I missed you." That was a real attention getter and I told him I felt the same way about him.

We were only about two and a half hours apart from each other but hardly saw each other or talked. At another wedding reception we both attended, Tom and I were seated at different tables. We were both seated with people we didn't know and we both wanted to at least sit with family. When everyone was finished eating Tom and I got together and talked for quite a while and also spent some time with other family members. I knew it was kind of unusual that we only talked when we saw each other at functions like that.
When Jeanne and I moved to York County, Tom and I would, every once in a while, talk on the phone when we could get hold of each other. There was a time in each of our lives when we weren't big telephone talkers so the conversations weren't as frequent as I wished they had been. But after I retired and moved to Texas, Tom and I talked more on the phone than we ever had before.

It was on one of those calls that Tom told me he was at a local garage getting his RV inspected. I told him I didn't know he had purchased an RV and he said that he and Julie were tired of sleeping in a tent on the ground when they went camping. They enjoyed camping during the summer months too much to give it up so they purchased a used RV. He explained how Julie had haggled with the dealer and got the price down to the range they were expecting to spend. I then knew if I called Tom on a summer weekend, he would be camping somewhere.

That's were Tom and I differed. I would tell him that after spending a year of sleeping on the ground when I was in Vietnam, I really had no interest in doing it now. Of course, if I was really that interested, I could have done what he and Julie had done and purchased an RV. But I had other interests.

After about a year in Texas, we decided to take a trip back to Altoona. We only had about three days there so we were really busy and had a lot of family to visit. I made sure I made one of those visits was to see Tom. It was only for a couple of hours but it was well worth it. About a year later, we made that trip again and this time we all gathered at Link's home on a Sunday following church and lunch. We sat and watched football and discussed a lot of stuff. It was one of the best visits we had had in years. On one of those visits, Tom was recovering from rotator cuff surgery.

Now, we did have that in common since I had, by that time, both right and left rotator cuffs repaired and cleaned up. We sat on the sofa at his house and talked for about three hours. His recovery was very similar to mine. Neither of us had experienced the excruciating pain that most people experience following that surgery. It must be in the genes. Some time following that trip, Tom called and told me he had a knee replacement. It was the same thing with that recovery; it was no time at all he was able to climb stairs and do it with no pain. Some people baby their knee and refuse to do the rehab but Tom moved forward at a rapid pace and without pain. But Tom had put on weight over the years and that caused him to have high blood pressure and a cholesterol problem. The doctor told him he would have to go on medication for both but Tom told him he would take care of it himself. And, he did. He dropped about forty pounds and his blood pressure and cholesterol numbers were both down and within acceptable ranges. Tom was doing steps and riding his bike and eating better.

I saw Tom in a video at a family member's funeral and he looked like a different person. He looked really good. He had dropped all that excess weight and looked like he did when he was a Marine. I was so disappointed that I couldn't be there for that funeral and to be able to talk with Tom in person. We had begun to talk more on the phone but it wasn't the same as talking in person. But I was so glad I got to see him in that video. That would be the last time I would see Tom on video or in person but we continued to talk by phone more frequently. Covid-19 had caused a pandemic and shut down the country. Traveling wasn't forbidden but the government had put extreme fear into far too many people. Businesses were shut down and trying to make a thirteen-hundred-mile trip was pretty dangerous. Hotels were closed and it was difficult to know if there were fuel stops available. Jeanne and I would have loved to have made another trip to the Altoona area but it wasn't worth the risk. So, Tom and I spoke more frequently on the phone.

Tom had discovered an interest in woodworking. Our brother Link had been involved in woodworking for years and was very good at the skill. I also enjoyed woodworking and built much of my own furniture and case goods like dressers, nightstands, beds and cabinets.

Link had built some very complicated projects and the items were perfect. So, Tom told me that he had built a toybox, I think it was a toybox, for a friend of theirs and was working on some other stuff. This was quite an accomplishment for Tom since he never appeared to have the skill for this type of work. As good of a welder as he was, he never explored much outside of that with any other craft. But he was pretty good at it. Our dad was a very talented guy when it came to building, repairing or fixing. He had to be because he couldn't afford to have anyone do it for him. So, I'm sure Tom and I both inherited that from him. It just took Tom a little longer to discover it. I always told him, "Don't worry. I can't weld and if I did, it wouldn't be very good and would probably always be a bubble gum weld.

One of the last times I talked with Tom, he was helping a man who was putting a metal shed together for him. He told me he was paying the guy to do it because he wasn't sure he knew how. But the man asked Tom if he would help him and Tom jumped in and discovered he could have done it but chalked it up as a learning experience.

Tom had to move on from his welding job because it was bothering his back. So, he went to work at Skills in Altoona. It is a state-run facility that works with mentally challenged people. That fit right into Tom's area of compassion and desire to help people. He had the patience for it. He would tell me about the guys he would work with who were challenged. He was to teach them minor skills and how to manage real life situations. One of Tom's responsibilities was driving a truck for pick ups and deliveries of various items. He would have one guy working with him and it was Tom's job to teach him how it all worked and to make sure he performed the duties he was assigned as he worked with Tom.

Tom told me that most of the guys he worked with were not a problem. But every once in a while, he would get one who just didn't want to cooperate. Tom had a special way of handling them. He simply had to be very stern and explain what they could expect if they didn't cooperate with him. He didn't go soft on the ones who wanted to rebel and he just laid down the law to them and they came around.

When the pandemic hit and the world walked around with masks on everywhere they went, it was the same with this state-run facility.

As long as Tom was in the facility, he had to have a mask on. Even after many businesses had stopped requiring masks, this state-run facility continued to require it. He told me he would go off of the property to eat his lunch so he could take his mask off. If he was attached to a client all day, he would tell him they were going outside to eat lunch.
Finally, he got tired of it and retired. He had been putting off retirement for a time but he decided it was time. He couldn't tolerate wearing the mask all day. His boss tried to talk him into staying but he wasn't having it. He retired and never regretted it. He was glad he had pulled the plug on his working days and began to enjoy retirement.

When that doctor told Tom about his blood pressure and cholesterol and Tom said he would take care of it, he did. But when Tom began to work out, he became somewhat obsessed with it. He lived in a two-story house and he would do the stairs in repetitions of twenty-five up and down. He would take his bike in the back of his truck to the Penn State campus in town and ride his bike around campus at night. He told me he had bought his daughter and his wife new bikes for Christmas even though his wife didn't ride. But he and his daughter, Crystal, would ride their bikes in the evening.
But Tom was over doing it. I had called him one day and he didn't answer. He returned my call that evening at about ten o'clock his time. He told me he was at the campus riding his bike because he had gained three pounds. I was quick to tell him not to get into that game of watching a few pounds here and there. He insisted he wasn't doing that and he just enjoyed riding his bike. It was ten o'clock at night! I told him I had done that same thing years before and then came to my senses and stopped worrying about one, two or three pounds. He insisted he wasn't doing that but Julie didn't agree. She told me he was pushing too hard.

I received a call on a Monday in late January 2022 from my nephew, Jim. I couldn't believe what he told me. I was shocked by what he said. He told me, "Uncle Bill, Uncle Tom had a heart attack." It took a little time for that message to sink in. I just couldn't believe my brother Tom had a heart attack and was fighting for his life. That was something I never expected to hear. Tom had lost the weight and was eating healthy and kept in good physical condition.

I began to pray for him and asked God to perform a miracle and keep him alive. But I also knew God's will was in play here and if it was His will that Tom would die, then that is what I was prepared for. When I spoke with Julie on the phone, she told me Tom had acted different when he got up that morning. First of all, she said he was always up before her and that morning he had slept in and got up after she did.
Julie said he went right into his routine of doing the steps and she was busy in the kitchen. It wasn't long after that when she heard a gasp and found Tom in a chair and not breathing. She had called 911 and they arrived quickly while she was doing CPR. They came in and took over and rushed him to the hospital which was only a few blocks away. By the time his heart began to beat again, he had been down for about thirty minutes. I didn't know that until after Tom died.
On the following Friday, Jim called again to tell me Tom had died. That call wasn't as surprising as the first. I had spoken to Julie that morning and she told me that they were going to pull the plug on Tom that day since there was no brain activity. I accepted that news.

The doctor told Julie that Tom's heart attack had been caused by a scaring on his heart from a previous heart attack. But Tom had never knew he had had a heart attack prior to this one. The doctor explained that is possible with a lot of people. He told her it had probably been so mild of a heart attack that Tom wasn't even aware of it but it had left this scar on his heart and the excessive workout Tom had been going through that morning caused the attack.

In one of our last phone conversations, I was explaining to Tom how the neuropathy in my feet was hampering my ability to do a lot of the stuff I used to do. I told him, "But I will never give up. I'm going to keep pushing and not allow this to stop me." He agreed and said he was doing the same. Little did I know that when I told him that, I was indirectly encouraging him to continue those strenuous workouts. I was asking myself, "Did I cause him to keep pushing so hard?" I was told it wouldn't have mattered if I told him that or not. He was going to keep up his routine. I told others that Tom was pushing himself like he was that 20 year-old Marine again. Tom was 69 when he died.

Epilog

For as far back as I can remember, Tom was always my best friend and was always there as my brother. As boys running around that farm where we lived for about five years and even as grown men, we were close brothers. I remember back to when we lived in Iselin as really young boys, and how dad used to sit Tom and me on a bench outside the basement door and cut some kind of fruit in pieces and give it to us to eat. We were always together. We played together and we fought with each other and our mom would always tell us, "The winner gets a beating." Of course, she didn't mean she was going to literally beat us. We understood that to mean the winner will be the one who gets spanked and we would immediately stop fighting.

Even as we grew up through our adolescent and teen years and our interests began to differ, we were still as close as ever. I was playing sports and Tom was playing the guitar. But we both had an interest in music and loved listening to the radio. If we were in the car with our mom, we would always turn the radio to our favorite station and turn it up. Then mom would calmly reach over and turn it down a little. With dad driving, I would turn the radio up a little but not a lot. I knew he didn't want it blaring in his ears while he was driving. And not only that, but our dad was a country music guy. Tom and I didn't really like country music but that would change in his adult years. I never did have a liking for country music.

Living on the farm, Tom and I shared a bedroom, as we had in Elders Ridge and at Nudge's. We never had a second thought about sharing a bedroom. After all, we only slept there and we never had any fights or disputes over anything concerning the bedroom. We had to share the same bed and we never had any disputes over that. But on the farm with all those stories about that house being haunted, Tom and I were glad we were in the same room and in the same bed.

Tom said he would turn his back facing away from the bed so he wouldn't see anything. I was the opposite. I would sleep facing away from the bed because I didn't want anything sneaking up on me. It all sounds silly now but to an 8 and 10 years old, it was serious business.

As I had mentioned earlier about Tom's compassion for strays, it wouldn't be fair not to mention how Tom never lost that compassion for people in need or who simply needed a friend. Tom and Julie took in Billy Paul Bernell and his mother and they lived with Tom and Julie for a while. But Billy Paul, as Tom used to refer to him, was attached to Tom and Tom was the male figure in his life. If Tom and Julie went somewhere, Billy Paul was there with them. The time I referred to when Jeanne and I met with Tom and Julie for breakfast in Lancaster, PA, Billy Paul was with them. Billy Paul grew up knowing Tom as a father figure and Tom treated him as a son. How many men do you know who would take in a boy and his mom and then continue to maintain a relationship with that boy as he grew into a young man? That's exactly what Tom did. Tom instilled some great qualities into this young man's life. Billy Paul, who now is simply referred to as Bill, learned how to play the guitar from Tom and he has just recently begun an enlistment in the Marines. This was the result of a strong influence from Tom and his love for the Corps.

We will never know how this young man's life would have turned out if it wasn't for Tom's influence on him. As I watched the video feed of Tom's funeral, I watched as Bill played one of the last songs Tom had written. It wasn't perfect and not as good as Tom would have played it but that wasn't the point. Bill played that song for Tom and was telling everyone that Tom had taught him so much more than just being a beginner guitar player. Thinking all the way back to Iselin and the stray dogs Tom would bring home to Bob Andrews in Blairsville, it was all a telling of Tom's compassion. Bob Andrews was a thorn in Tom's side at times but Tom could never tell Bob to just go away. Tom was Bob's big brother and even though Bob became like one of the family because he spent so much time with us, Tom was still the one member of the family who Bob was attached to. And that compassion stayed with Tom right up to and through his time at Skills before he retired. Tom just couldn't say no to someone in need.

Tom was a loving father. He fought hard to get his daughter away from a woman who was unqualified to be a mother. Yes, she gave birth to Crystal but she was never able to be a loving mother. The woman was mentally challenged and so is Crystal and required special care which the mother couldn't and wasn't able to provide. Tom sacrificed a lot in his life to get custody of and then provide for his daughter. He knew and was aware of her needs and he made sure she got them. And, he did a great job of raising her. She is a wonderful and pleasant woman now.
Tom, as I mentioned earlier, would make sure she got to work at four in the morning and even latter in life when she would get off at 11 PM, he would make sure she had a ride home. He wasn't a helicopter parent by any means. He simply provided for and took care of his daughter like any loving father would have. Crystal was born on Christmas day and I always used to kid her about the difference in birthday presents and Christmas presents. I would ask her if she received double the number of gifts and Tom was quick to jump in and say, "No. We simply set some aside and told her those were the birthday presents and the rest are Christmas presents." Then, I would tease her and tell her she was getting cheated because her birthday was on Christmas and didn't get as many gifts. Then she agreed with me but Tom ended that argument really quick.

While we were still living in York County PA, Tom called me one night and told me Crystal had something she wanted to ask me and he put her on the phone. I could tell she was a little nervous and then she asked, "Uncle Bill, will you marry Robert and me? Will you do our wedding?" At first, I was a little bit stunned. I never realized that she and Robert were even considering marriage. I guess when I thought of Crystal, I always seen her in my mind as that young girl who was always attached to her dad. I had met Robert and talked to him on a few occasions but just never thought of the two of them marrying. My answer to her was yes but told her I wanted to talk to her and Robert together which is something I always do before marrying any man and woman.

Tom told me she had wanted him to ask if I would do the ceremony and he told her she had to do it. That's just a small example of how Tom was a teaching father to her. He taught her everything she needed to know about life. He did an excellent job.

I did do Crystal's and Robert's wedding and almost screwed it up but most people didn't catch it. I had instructed Robert and Crystal to simply relax and not to even think about the people being there. I was trying to keep them from being too nervous and to simply follow me. Well, the pages of my little black book where the wedding ceremony and vows were printed stuck together and without realizing I went from an early part of the ceremony to the latter part. Robert caught it right away and I just motioned for him to play along and I was able to adlib and get them through it.
I had asked Tom and Crystal at the rehearsal if they knew whether Patty, Crystal's birth mother, was going to come. Tom said he didn't think she would come and when I asked Crystal, "What will you do if your mom shows up?" Her answer was quick, "Julie is my mom." That settled that.

Tom was a man who was very simple in his life. He was content with what he had. If he only had a few dollars in his pocket, he was content. If he couldn't afford something, he simply moved on. He was satisfied, most of the time, with the work he did and whoever he was working for. Tom always had enough as far as he was concerned. He didn't cheat or cut corners to get anything. He worked hard and many times for far less than he should have earned but he was satisfied. I had often wished that I could have been as content as he was in many parts of life. He was very much like his dad in those areas.
Tom could make friends with anyone and at the same time, if you gave him any flack, he could take care of himself and give it right back. But for the most part, if you couldn't be friends with Tom, you had personal problems. He was always well thought of and appreciated. From his school years right up until the day he died, Tom was always well thought of by those who knew him.

When Tom lived with Link in his teen years, he was like a big brother to Link's sons, Ken and Jim. Tom taught them how to wrestle and took care of them like a big brother. Tom was more of a brother to Ken and Jim then an uncle. He was right there with them at home. He helped them with a lot of things and they looked up to Tom and considered him as their big brother. I was always so happy for Tom when Link took him in and gave him a home and a family. It was the best thing that could have happened to him.

When Tom died and moved on to be with Jesus, it was like a part of me died too. In recent times, Tom and I would call each other frequently. If I thought of something I considered he would want hear, I would call him and he would do the same. I wrote a book about three years ago and based it on the antics of our childhood. I would call Tom to clarify events or times and we would put our heads together and figure it out. The book was fiction based on fact.[1] If he had a question, he would just call me and we would talk about it.

And if either of us missed a call, we would be sure to return it. I just never imagined what life would be like if Tom wasn't around or if I couldn't talk to him. Our conversations about our childhood and growing up and also about our time in the Marines is certainly missed. I still have those times when something will come to my mind and I think about calling Tom but then reality hits me and I realize I can't do that anymore.

I miss my brother dearly and so many times I wish I could pick up my phone and talk to him about those things we always talked about. In many ways, he was so much better at life than I am. But that's the way God made him and I was made differently and I can accept that. But what is comforting is that I know I will see him again. I also know there are many people who scoff at that and think it is just a way we make ourselves feel better after the death of a loved one. But I know it is true and I look forward to the day when I can meet him there with Jesus.

> ***There is more than enough room in my Father's home. If this were not so, would I have told you that I am going to prepare a place for you.***
>
> ***Jesus Christ, John 14:2, The Holy Bible, NLT***

There is so much more I could have written about Tom. But that would require volumes. I hope you enjoyed what I have written.

---

[1] *Growing Up Simple, Bill Petite, Amazon*

www.ingramcontent.com/pod-product-compliance
Lightning Source LLC
LaVergne TN
LVHW050602160826
845677LV00011B/2419

9798367784428